Republic F-105
Thunderchief

OSPREY AIR COMBAT

Republic F-105
Thunderchief

DAVID ANDERTON

91745

Published in 1983 by Osprey Publishing Limited
12-14 Long Acre, London WC2E 9LP
Member company of the George Philip Group

Sole distributors for the USA

Motorbooks International
Publishers & Wholesalers Inc
Osceola, Wisconsin 54020, USA

British Library Cataloguing in Publication Data

Anderton, David
  Republic F-105 Thunderchief. – (Osprey air combat)
  1. Thunderchief (Fighter planes)
  I. Title
  623.74'63   TL685.3
ISBN 0-85045-530-8

 Originated and produced by
Anchor Books Limited, Bournemouth, Dorset

Photosetting by Poole Typesetting (Wessex) Limited,
Bournemouth, Dorset
Page Film by Aero Offset (Bournemouth) Limited,
Bournemouth, Dorset
Colour separations by Apperley Graphics Limited,
Parkstone, Dorset
Printed in England by
BAS Printers, Over Wallop,
Hampshire

Contents

Foreword

Fighter pilots tend to take their machines for granted. They're very good, or good, or, once in a while, not so good. The performance of pilot and aircraft soon forms an image in public and private minds, while the struggles of those who created that machine are largely ignored. The machine gives of itself until, through one cause or another, it can give no more and dies – dashed to ignominious pieces on some stranger's mountainside, or damned to eternal broiling sun in a desert bone yard. An occasional war story brings it back to life, but for most of us, it's on to new sleeker, faster, more potent machinery.

A strange candidate to challenge this continuing rotation is the F-105, the Thud, so named by its early pilots because if you were careless enough to ignore its sheer mass, it would indeed contact the runway with an alarming thud. What could there be about an aircraft, sold as a nuclear-weapons delivery vehicle, that could excite a single-engined-fighter jock? It seemed at first that The Foundry had come up with another Lead Sled, larger, heavier and even less suitable for a rat race than its antecedents: The Hog, the Super Hog, and the Ultra Hog.

However, while the Thud was putting in its time, pretty well on its way to being replaced by the likes of the F-4C, something not so different happened. We decided to go for another no-win war, to see how much we could waste without really offending anybody on the other side; and who wound up in the forefront of the air war over south-east Asia? You betcha, the Thud.

Thus began a strange romance with the Thud, by the guys who daily hurled their pink bodies – and their Thuds – against Hanoi and by the guys who devoted their lives and skills to pasting the broken birds back together again. They all forgot that nuke stuff and vegetating on a five minute alert, forgot that the south-east Asia war plan was full of holes. It was fighter-pilot time. The defenses were the fiercest ever known to man. The bullets were real. Real, nice, people were being killed or doomed to living hell in Hanoi prisons every day. And center stage, there she was the Thud.

She changed character. We found out that we could load her down so she could barely get out of the chocks, yet that huge burner would deliver the brute force to hurl her into the air from a jungle airfield on a sweltering, calm day. We found out we could hold the force together while staggering inbound through thunderstorms that arched high above 50,000 feet and through rain that reduced the guy on your wingtip to a single red or green Christmas-tree

light. Out of the strong will to survive we found tankers, and refueled, in junk like that.

When we got there, we found we could nudge Mach 1 on the deck, and she wouldn't come apart despite bumps and twists you wouldn't believe. If you haven't experienced that, you've missed what maximum performance truly means. We could put the bombs right where we wanted, we could beat the MiGs, and – despite the awesome odds – a lot of us got back with battle damage you had to see to believe. Let's face it: It was a rotten war whose over-supervision and restrictions made it even worse, but the Thud performed with honor throughout.

So with the war over for many years, now, the few Thuds still flying with the AF Reserve are about due to get their bones bleached in an Arizona junk yard, and it's all part of aerial history, right? Wrong. The few Thuds still flying are treated like ageless sex symbols. The reunions increase, the historical interest increases, and the Thud refuses to go away. She has firmly established herself in the heart of fighter-aviation's strongest proponents. That, and the devotion of those who created her, is what this book is all about.

For me, admiration comes easily. The first fighter I strapped to my butt was a Republic P-47. I lived through the pains of the early F-84s and early F-105s. I gloried in leading the Thunderbirds in show after show in the polished versions of the straight-winged and swept-winged F-84s. I looked at the first mock-up of the Thud, and listened to Alexander Kartveli dream out loud. I watched people like Mundy Peale and Ken Ellington scheme to make the machine a reality. I watched men like Jimmie Roye burn themselves out trying to force the concept into being.

It did become reality. The process of perfection wasn't fast, nor was it easy, as you will see in the pages that follow; but the record is clear. The Thud went where nobody else wanted to go, or could go. The people who flew and supported that proud beauty will never forget her, or the people who created her. The thrill of flying a good machine in support of your Nation's objectives just will not go away, nor will reminiscences of the Thud.

Colonel Jack Broughton USAF (Retd)
LANCASTER
California 1983

Introduction

If ever an aircraft needed to prove and reprove the formulae for flight, it was the Republic F-105 Thunderchief. It's a commonplace to recite its derogatory nicknames. Those names, were awarded by those who never flew the Thud, the nickname most generally accepted by her pilots. If you were fortunate enough to fly her, you named her 'Iron Butterfly', or 'Big Sal', or 'The Great Speckled Bird'. She was also the 'Hanoi Hustler', 'Takhli Taxi', 'The Two-Baht Bus', 'Ridge-Runner', and 'Red River Raider'.

She had her admitted faults. Designed to do one job exceptionally well, she – happily – never had to do it with a live nuclear weapon. Instead, she filled roles she had not been built for – some that didn't exist when she was planned. She bore the brunt of bombing missions in the long and bitter war in south-east Asia. She tempted enemy defenses, playing a deadly game at the very real risk of being eaten alive by a salvo of SAMs (surface-to-air missiles), or a burst of 23-mm automatic, radar-directed cannon fire. When all the statistics were in, they showed that she had flown more than three-quarters of the bombing missions into North Vietnam.

She was a remarkable, extraordinary aircraft, a brilliant design, a synthesis of artistry and brute force, Beauty and the Beast simultaneously. She had a fine figure, a sensuous shape with gently curving waist. Her wings seemed too small, but they, too, curved in an exciting arc. She slashed through the fiery air faster than any other tactical aircraft of her time and decades later could still outrun friend or foe alike on the deck. Brute power would thrust her, protesting, through the angry skies, but she could skitter along just above the nap of the earth, and you never heard her coming until the shock wave slammed at your skin, shotgunned your ears and heralded her rapid departure over the next ridge.

She was born out of the experiences and philosophies of one war to become an integral part of another. She was flown by certified heroes, and not all of them received Medals of Honor or Silver Stars. The whine of the powerful jet engine rises to a tortured scream and then a hoarse roar. Ponderously, the heavy Thunderchief begins to roll into the light wind that is blowing straight on to the nose. A sudden thunderclap announces the afterburner and the plane accelerates. Along the runway's black surface it streaks, ogival nose directly over the white centreline, holding on a distant point.

Lights and markers flash by and still it rolls, engine howling, red-orange diamonds stabilized in the bright foxtail of the afterburner exhaust. The nose starts to lift; the craft rotates about its mainwheels smoothly, gently, and the shock struts extend as the heavyweight hulk finally is borne more on its wings than on its wheels.

And then it is up, flying, into its medium, landing gear swinging through arcs to slam into the wheel wells as the boundary of the field slips underneath. A continuing cacophony echoes across the countryside, bounces back from the low hills to the east. The sleek ship gathers speed, streaking across the soft land below, climbing steadily on an invisible ramp of bright air. For long seconds its thunder continues, then, finally softening, blends into the background noise and disappears.

Many who flew her died with her, others are listed as missing in action. Those who flew her came back with her have stories to tell for a lifetime of squadron reunions and generations of grandchildren.

David A. Anderton
Rigewood, New Jersey, 1983

1
One More Thunderstorm

An aircraft weapons system is designed and developed within the context of its times. Its lines may be sketched on the back of an envelope, or detailed on the screen of a computer terminal. Its geometry may involve the intuitive inspiration of a single designer, or the collective ideas of dozens. It may be proposed to the Air Force, Navy or Army in the few pages of an informal letter, or in the thousands of pages of a whole mass of reports. However, it has not been conceived in a technical vacuum, carried during gestation in ignorance of the outside world, and delivered finally free of original sin. Quite the contrary.

At each stage of its development, that aircraft has been influenced by factors that range from the geopolitical state of the entire world to the love-life of the responsible military officer. Local and national politics play important parts, as do the policies of the manufacturers, the military and the government. The mood of the voters, the strength of the trades union movement and the balance of power in Congress play a part, while sabre-rattling, the return of political favors owed and pockets of unemployment affect the final decision to buy a fighter or a bomber.

Once chosen, the life of the contracted aircraft may not run smoothly. Look specifically at the F-105. In less than four years from receipt of a letter contract, procurement of that aircraft had been authorised, drastically cut, suspended, timidly reinstated, slashed to a trio of planes, generously doubled to six, increased to 15 of three different models, further increased to 82 of two models and then cancelled for one model. Twice, the situation changed within a one-month period; the longest era of stability was 13 months. At least twice, Republic requested schedule

The second prototype YF-105A now named 'Thunderchief'

stretches because of its own slippages in development and production, and the Air Force announced a third elongation. A strike shut the factory down for ten weeks. The fleet was grounded four times within two and a half years, after establishing what was claimed as a new record for a tactical fighter by completing its first operational year without a single major accident.

The F-105 missed its target date for IOC (Initial Operational Capability) by four years, more than doubling the planned time span; and yet, when the F-105 went to war, it stayed there for seven years of combat missions. Further, it lasted in service with active United States Air Force units until nearly 30 years after it had been ordered (that's like having Eddie Rickenbacker's beloved SPADs in service from World War I through World War II).

The F-105 Thunderchief was a great beast of an aircraft, standing so high off the ground that only very athletic pilots could manage to touch the wing leading edge. Its take-off weight for combat missions was

almost 25 tons. It stretched nearly 65 feet from the tip of its radome to the trailing edge of the petal speed brakes. The tip of its vertical tail towered 20 feet above the ground. To hold it in the air, Republic had provided what seemed like a ridiculously small wing, measuring only 385 square feet in area, sweeping back 45 degress measured along the quarter-chord line and producing wing loadings that were close to 130 pounds per square foot at take-off.

It was designed originally as a single-purpose weapon, a supersonic fighter-bomber capable of carrying an internally stored nuclear-fission weapon at speeds in excess of Mach 1 at sea level. Its survival was to be in its speed and low-altitude performance; it was not expected to be a figher, to mix with the MiGs, one versus one, in contrail country. Indeed, as the F-105 was stretched into the F-105F and F-105G two-seaters, it became unable to climb to the 30,000-foot level, falling short by about a mile or more, depending on the loading of fuel and weapons.

In spite of its accepted deficiency as a fighter, it turned in a surprising performance once it got into combat in the hands of experienced pilots who knew that guns really weren't obsolete offensive weapons. Enemy fliers found that out; 28 of them, driving MiG-17s, were blasted out of the sky by F-105 pilots.

By the time the G model arrived on the scene, with its advanced Wild Weasel gear, the Vietnam War was winding down and so was the F-105's performance. The design by then was 20 years old. The weight of the F-105G had risen to more than 52,000 pounds at take-off on a combat mission, a figure that approached the equivalent weight of the famous World War II four-engined Boeing B-17E. It climbed at 2,900 feet per minute, hardly a sparkling performance. After 28 minutes it could reach 30,000 feet, but it took all the

old girl had to get there. It stalled at 188 knots, power off and in the landing condition. Its unrefuelled combat radius was under 400 miles, and its take-off distance was more than 8,000 feet.

The story of the Republic F-105 begins in 1951, when Harry S. Truman was President of the United States and the country was embroiled in a war in Korea. The Chinese Air Force held temporary air superiority in 'MiG Alley', soon to lose it to the North American F-86 Sabres of the 4th and 51st Fighter Interceptor Wings. The USAF had ordered its first cruise missile, the subsonic Martin B-61A Matador. Grumman was building straight-winged F9F-2 Panthers, Lockheed was delivering F-94 Starfires. McDonnell was producing F2H-2 Banshees for the Navy and about to deliver its planned

The ancestry of the F-105 is clearly seen here, by the shape of the fuselage nose, the wing and inlet, also the vertical tail, in the early production F-84F (foreground) and RF-84F

successor, the ill-starred XF3H-1 Demon. Vought was building its old bent wing bird, the F4U-7, last of the piston-engined fighters of World War II still in production. In that year, too, the Lockheed XC-130 design won a USAF competition for a tactical transport. Convair received a contract to design a nuclear-powered aircraft and the USAF announced development of tactical nuclear weapons for use against ground troops. Pratt & Whitney was working on a new and powerful jet engine, the J57.

Republic Aviation Corporation, of Farmingdale, Long Island, New York, was turning its efforts to a $580-million backlog of production orders for the F-84E and F-84G Thunderjet, a pair of straight-winged fighter-bombers performing ably in the Korean War. The F-84F Thunderstreak, a swept-wing version of improved performance, had made its first flight.

Kartveli was a Russian emigrant born in Tbilisi, Georgia (now the Georgian SSR), Josef Stalin's hometown. A serving officer in Word War I; he was wounded in action, then sent by the Georgian government to Paris to study French military tactics. He was there when the Revolution ripped his country apart, leaving him stranded in Paris. To support himself, he taught mathematics and performed as a trapeze artist, while acquiring degrees in both aeronautical and electrical engineering.

He was recruited to work in the United States, at Columbia Aircraft Corporation, by Charles A. Levine, an aviation promoter and investor. Levine was a millionaire and a former scrap dealer who had made history, in a way, by flying across the Atlantic as a passenger with Clarence Chamberlain in June 1927. Kartveli worked for Columbia for a while, then left to go to Atlantic Aircraft Corporation, the US licensee for Fokker aircraft.

When Alexander de Seversky, another Russian emigrant, organized his own company in early 1931, Kartveli went with him as Chief Engineer. He had been with Republic and its predecessor, the Seversky Aircraft Corporation, since that date. As Chief Engineer, his influence on design and designers was great. He made major contributions to a whole line of Seversky/Republic aircraft that were known for high cruise speed and long range: the SEV-1XP, SEV-2XP, BT-8 and SEV-3 and the chubby pre-war pursuit, the P-35. He had been part of the team that revised and developed a single basic airframe, common to all those designs, into the XP-41, YP-43 and P-44. Some of its features even survived in the famed P-47 Thunderbolt of World War II.

Associates remember his contributions to the F-105 program as primarily the exertion of early leadership and later suggestions, with not too much direct input or influence on the final design and development.

The Air Force, which had successfully made its case for independence and the doctrine of strategic bombing, was frustrated by the war in Korea. There were no strategic targets left after a couple of weeks, but contrary to the doctrine so vigorously promulgated by General Henry H. Arnold and other proponents of strategic bombing, including Alexander de Seversky – the Koreans were not waving the white flag. Further, the 'backward peasants' of North Korea, admittedly aided and abetted by their Russian and Chinese allies, were making high-altitude level bombing a suicide mission.

The final answer, discovered after considerable loss, was that low-level strikes by fighter-bombers were a better way to conduct that kind of war. The planes went in low and fast, dropping bombs and napalm, firing rockets and strafing. Back in the United States, a lot of thought was being devoted to finding solutions to the problems of the next war, modulated by the temporising solutions of the Korean affair.

With Kartveli dead and living memories blurred by the passage of 30 years, we may never know the exact steps that led to the lines on paper defining the shape and performance of the F-105. The Korean war experience certainly was one major influence. The underpowered performance of the late-model F-84 was another. The development of a tactical nuclear fission weapon, smaller than the Hiroshima and Nagasaki bombs, was a third.

Any aircraft company looks to extend its existing production line for as long a time as possible. It makes economic sense and if extra performance can be added through modifications to the basic airframe the company stands a good chance of getting follow-on orders from the military. Logically, then, Kartveli and Republic were studying a stretched, or modified, or improved F-84. The F-84F was a sleek, swept-wing aircraft, using the first generation of that aerodynamic technology. It was underpowered, but it had a rugged airframe with the promise of increased performance if larger engines could be fitted. That modification – increased engine power – is almost the first one studied. At the same time, a company design team likes to look ahead to the development of an entirely new type of aircraft, starting with clean rolls of tracing paper. So, when Kartveli and his closest associates were not engrossed in modifying the F-84F, they were undoubtedly thinking about designing an entirely new fighter, using the technology that had been learned since World War II and adding as leavening the experiences of the Korean war.

William O'Donnell, one of Kartveli's close associates, remembers one factor contributing to the F-105 evolution. The USAF felt that a specific tactical nuclear weapon, intended for the F-84 series, ought to be carried in a bomb bay rather than on the wings or fuselage centreline (that weapon was referred to at Republic as the Douglas shape, its external lines having been developed by Douglas Aircraft Company in a series of studies and tests to develop low-drag aircraft bomb shapes). Republic designers laid out a bomb bay for the F-84F; it was geometrically possible but the added weight of structure around the fuselage cut-out and the addition of bomb racks and other equipment would have seriously degraded the F-84F'

performance, given its available power.

Republic continued to study the problem with Tactical Air Command (TAC) and with the Air Force Special Weapons Center at Kirtland AFB, New Mexico. The sketches and calculations produced an overall design concept that met the requirements for an advanced F-84F but was dependent on the availability of a more powerful engine.

One possible engine choice was the General Electric J73, then the power plant for the North American F-86H Sabre. It was scheduled for installation in a modified Republic F-84F airframe, later redesignated the YF-84J, as a means of increasing the performance of that aircraft. O'Donnell said that the very first design for the AP-63, Republic's original project designation for what became the F-105, was planned around the J73 engine (O'Donnell also pointed out that the AP designation – for Army Proposal – was a hangover from the old days at Seversky, when the company was preparing both Army and Navy designs and gave them either an AP or NP identifier).

However, the GE powerplant, then in short supply and having troubles, was never developed in to the advanced model that Republic wanted for the AP-63 proposal. As alternatives, the company considered both the Allison J71 and the Wright J67. The former was the production engine for the twin-jet Douglas B-66 Destroyer (USAF version of the Douglas A-3D Skywarrior series for the Navy) and the latter was the British Bristol Olympus, licensed to Wright.

Meanwhile, remembers Murray Berkow, another Kartveli associate, Pratt & Whitney was '...coming along with the J57 and we went out to Wright-Patterson to talk to those people (Wright Air Development Center) about putting the J57 in the F-84F. That led to a design study which resulted in a F-84F lengthened to compensate for the larger engine. This craft was heavier, so it required a new wing – and when the balance was again adjusted, there was room for a bomb bay after all.

So Republic apparently had two or more roughly parallel design studies in progress, involving the

ABOVE RIGHT
A Republic model of Army Proposal 63. Note that it has the F-84F inlets and general shape, and that it carries unguided air-to-ground rockets for the tactical support mission

CENTRE RIGHT
This Republic model looks exactly like the AP-63, but is labeled F-105. Both models were shown by Republic during May, 1958, by which time the F-105D was nearing final approval. The wing is shown with leading-edge flaps outboard, conventional large-span ailerons. The F-105 retained the former, but changed to short-span outboard ailerons

RIGHT
Republic made a series of wind-tunnel tests to study the problem of dropping bombs. This model shows a retractable windbreak at the front of the bomb bay

collective efforts of about 15 engineers. One design undoubtedly was a larger, higher-performance F-84F, powered by a Pratt & Whitney J57 and capable of carrying a fission weapon in an internal bomb bay. The other was the early outline or outlines of an entirely new aircraft, the AP-63, planned around the GE J73 power plant. The Air Force may have considered both design options at the time: the military, like the manufacturers, wants to keep existing production going as long as possible.

Accordingly to O'Donnell, it was the latter aircraft (AP-63) which was submitted to the USAF in a Republic proposal during February 1952, but by the time the contract was being written, the J73 engine had been replaced by the Allison J71. AP-63 had a clear advantage over another modification, however improved, of the ageing F-84 design. AP-63 was new, with a promised major performance margin over the existing F-84F. It had a bomb bay for internal carriage of the fission weapon; it promised supersonic speed at low altitude and already the advantages of that method of attacking a well defended enemy had become obvious.

The Air Staff, advised by the Aircraft and Weapon Board, gave consent to the project in May 1952, choosing the option of a new aircraft rather than a modified and improved F-84F. In September, Republic received a letter contract for the development and production of 199 F-105 aircraft, with a scheduled Initial Operational Capability (IOC) of 1955. The F-105 was to be one of the first USAF aircraft developed under the weapons system concept. WS-306A (its weapons system identifier) was to be placed almost entirely under the control of Republic; the company would be responsible for integrating the aircraft, its sub-systems – including test and ground-support equipment – and its GFAE (Government-Furnished Aircraft Equipment). In the future, if anything went wrong with the F-105 or any of its systems, Republic was the place where corrective action would have to begin.

The first official announcement of the program by the Air Force said that the engine would be the J71-A-7, developed by the Allison Division of General Motors. In March 1953, the contract was amended to reduce the procured quantity to 37 F-105s and nine RF-105s, the latter being a reconnaissance version of the basic aircraft, with cameras mounted in the nose.

The mock-up was ready for inspection in October 1953 and easily passed with no major changes. Problems had begun with the Allison J71 by then and the word was that it would not meet the thrust requirement for the F-105. As an interim choice, Republic planned to use the P&W J57 and then switch to the J71 when that engine came up to the thrust specification. The company still expected to meet both its delivery commitments and the IOC date of 1955.

Towards the end of 1953, the Air Force cancelled the entire program because of development delays at

Some basic aerodynamic characteristics show well here: Low-set horizontal tail (stabilator), ventral fin for increased stability at high angles of attack, thin wing and tail surfaces. This is the first YF-105A, 54-0098, on the dry lake bed at Edwards AFB

Republic. It was the start of a long period during which F-105 production was subjected to a series of procurement changes and uncertainties about the future of the aircraft. In February 1954, the program was reinstated with funding for 15 F-105 aircraft fitted with yet another engine, the powerful Pratt & Whitney J75. A single test aircraft was to be modified first for installation and testing of the larger power plant.

That change came about, said Berkow, because the YF-105A model was getting heavier and heavier with the addition of all the systems that the Air Force believed desirable for the role. 'So we went to Pratt & Whitney and asked them for a new engine; they adapted the J75 to fit in the F-105. They got the money to do it from the F-105 program.'

Also in February 1954, while the USAF was reinstating procurement of the F-105 and specifying the J75 engine for the airframe, a small group of officers inspected the mock-up of the reconnaissance version, the RF-105, at the Republic factory. They found little wrong, and gave their approval to the continuing development of the sub-type.

On 28 June, the contract was further revised. the 15

Although this is the first prototype, 54-0098, the basic outline of the Thunderchief remained unchanged to the end

aircraft ordered earlier that year were redefined as two YF-105As, powered by the P&W J57 engine, ten F-105Bs and three RF-105Bs, the latter two models to be equipped with the higher-thrust P&W J75. By September, however, continuing developmental delays caused the Air Force to slash the order to an insulting trio of aircraft, although a month later, perhaps seeing a need for a larger quantity of planes, the number was doubled.

Up to this point, Republic and the Air Force had been working from contractor specifications and an assumed requirement for the F-105. In USAF procedures at that time, a General Operational Requirement (GOR) defined aircraft missions and other desired performance and capabilities. It was customarily issued before the design had begun and not after the fact, but this time GOR 49 was issued on 1 December 1954, 31 months after the AP-63 design had received the go-ahead from the Air Staff. Berkow believes that the requirement was, in fact, written around the F-105B (that has been a common practice in the procurement of aircraft and it's regarded as legal, ethical and proper).

That GOR was based on a January 1951 set of characteristics for a fighter-bomber, amended in January 1952 and published in late 1953, a year and a half after the selection of the F-105. GOR 49 itself was to be amended three times over the next four months. It specified that the F-105 should be powered by the P&W J75 engine and that an advanced fire-control system and in-flight refuelling capability be added. The goal was to make the F-105 suitable for first-line service from 1958, the revised IOC date, through to 1960.

Two months later, in February 1955, the USAF authorised two prototype F-105A, 10 F-105B, and three RF-105 aircraft. This was the same distribution of types as had constituted the order for 15 aircraft placed a year earlier, but this batch was being procured under what was then known as the concept of concurrency, also called the Cook-Craigie plan, developed in the late 1940s by Generals Laurence C. Craigie, Deputy Chief of Staff/Development, and Orval R. Cook, DCS/Materiel.

The purpose of concurrency was to reduce the time between the start of a program and the achievement of the IOC, and the way to do that, it was believed then, was to go right into production. The first dozen or so aircraft off the line would be dedicated test aircraft. They would undergo an accelerated test program intended to detect problems soon enough so that solutions could be incorporated into early production aircraft.

'Rusty' Roth takes-off in the first prototype YF-105A. The flight went completely to plan and lasted for about 45 minutes. The date 22 October 1955

Concurrency made two optimistic assumptions, both wrong if history is any guide. The first is that only minor problems will turn up in early testing. The second is that detailed production drawings and tooling will be available from the start of the program. What frequently happened under the concurrency plan was that the early problems were too difficult to be solved in time to correct them in a preliminary stage of production. So it was to be with the F-105. That aircraft became the subject of several very expensive retrofit and modification programs, but the initial schedule slippage was probably responsible for saving some money, in a rather unusual way. If the early aircraft had been delivered on time, more of them would have been powered by the J57 engine. The result would have been a much larger number of nearly useless aircraft to dispose of afterwards.

The first two aircraft built carried serial numbers 54-0098 and 54-0099, and the official designation of YF-105A. They had airframes that – seen now in retrospect – resembled a cross between the F-84F and the F-105B geometries. The engine inlets were subsonic elliptical types similar to those of the F-84F. The vertical tail was of considerably smaller area

(approximately 79 percent of the size of production surfaces) and of lower height, aspect ratio, and sweepback angle when compared to the F-105B vertical surface. The fuselage of the YF-105A was 2 feet shorter, 1 foot narrower, and 3 inches shallower than that of the B model.

The powerplant finally used in the two YF-105As was the Pratt & Whitney J57-P-25. It was the same basic engine as the J57-P-21 in production for the North American F-100 Super Sabre, with two detail differences. First, the engine exhaust nozzle was extended by 22 inches in an afterburner flap-type nozzle. Second, the afterburner control unit was mounted on the side of the P-25 engine. Only six of the engines were ever assembled.

The J57-P-25 developed 16,000 pounds of thrust with afterburning, under sea-level static conditions. Its military rating was 10,200 pounds; continuous thrust rating was 8,700 pounds, and 90 percent cruise thrust was 7,800 pounds.

The J57 series featured two compressors in series, mechanically independent, with a drive turbine attached to each. The nine-stage low-pressure compressor was driven by a two-stage low-pressure turbine. The seven-stage high-pressure compressor was driven by a single-stage high-pressure turbine. The engine weighed about 4,200 pounds, was 155 inches long without afterburner and had a 39-inch diameter. It was first run in June 1949 and first developed its

10,000-pound design thrust in January 1950, and was first used on the eight-engined Boeing YB-52 Stratofortress.

By the time the pair were about to ready to fly, Republic knew that the YF-105A models were not representative of what the F-105 could, or would, be, but there was a schedule to meet, and appearances to maintain for the company and the Air Force, and so the project continued at full speed. It had been decided to fly the two prototypes first from the facilities of the Air Force Flight Test Center at Edwards AFB, California. It was a secure location and a safer one than surburban Long Island, with its housing developments that almost surrounded the Republic airfield.

Immediately after the final shop completion, the first YF-105A was readied for shipment. Engine runs and

ground checks were to be done at Edwards; Republic delivered the aircraft without even having checked whether or not the engine would start. Crews from the experimental shop at Republic went to Edwards to assist in the pre-flight and flight tests.

The first YF-105A (54-0098) lifted off the runway at Edwards on its maiden flight on 22 October 1955, at about the time that in-service F-105s were supposed to be strengthening the active units of the Air Force. Republic later claimed that it was flown a month ahead of schedule, without specifying what schedule. When the company's chief experimental test pilot, Russell M. Roth, who was never called anything but 'Rusty', completed the 45-minute first flight, he is reported to have said, 'A very fine ride, gentlemen.'

The Republic press release also claimed that the YF-105A exceeded Mach 1 on that 'very fine ride'. It

BELOW
The second YF-105A first flew on 28 January 1956. Shown here on a flight out of Edwards AFB, to test the aircraft's in-flight refuelling capabilities

could not have been by much, given the power available and the transonic drag of the YF-105A. That drag level was then unrelieved by the application of the NACA area rule that would later be required to make the F-105B a truly supersonic aircraft.

On 16 December 1955, the YF-105A was performing a series of high-speed runs to evaluate manoeuvring stability. The tests included straight-and-level dashes followed by high-*g* turns and a complete roll. After several successful runs, the plane was travelling at approximately 530 knots and was in a 5.5-*g* turn preparatory to the 360-degree roll when the right main landing gear suddenly extended and was torn off. Pilot 'Rusty' Roth brought the damaged bird back to the runway at Edwards, its left and nose landing gears retracted and its right wheel well empty and mangled. He held the aircraft off in a near stall as

long as he could, to slow the YF105A for landing. The tail section touched first, but then the nose dropped and hit the runway hard enough to break the back of the aircraft.

The first YF-105A had logged a total of 22 hours flight time, then was returned to the factory to be repaired. History is mute about its fate. The second YF-105A first flew on 28 January 1956 and it too disappeared into history. Both aircraft did contribute to the F-105's development. They were used for the flight evaluation of subsonic performance, handling qualities and manoeuvrability and – in so doing – saved some time from the already hard-pressed schedule. However, there was still a long road to travel before the F-105 could begin to meet the requirements of GOR 49, and before it could be called a fighter.

2
Clouds and Lightning

The experimental YF-105As had flown, proving little except that a large aircraft designed with contemporary technology could do so. The aircraft, envisioned as a supersonic fighter-bomber and procured as a weapons system, was far from either at that stage of its development. Its performance was barely supersonic and – even though additional thrust was expected from a new model of engine – its transonic drag was high enough to flag a warning to company aerodynamicists. Basically, the design was sound, but it was clear that much had yet to be done to make it an acceptable fighter-bomber. The first step had been completed; the basic aeroplane could fly. The next step was to make it perform to meet the requirements. The last step, still some years away, was to make it a fighter-bomber.

Republic had issued two specifications in August 1955, describing the F-105 powered by a J75-P-5 engine, and the RF-105 (then known under the designation of AP-71), a day photo-reconnaissance fighter dimensionally a replica of the F-105. It was to these two specifications that design of F-105 production aircraft had begun. The fighter, defined RAC Specification ES-349, was to weigh 23,873 pounds empty. Its maximum useful load totalled 20,580 pounds, including its Mk 7 nuclear store at 1,678 pounds. The corresponding maximum take-off weight was 44,453 pounds. At its design gross weight of 31,392 pounds, and with no external stores, the limit load factors were $+8\cdot67$ and $-4\,g$ for subsonic manoeuvring, and $+7\cdot33$ and $-3\,g$ for supersonic manoeuvring. The F-105 was nothing if not strong; few combat aircraft, before or since, have been designed for those kinds of structural limits.

The powerplant of the F-105 was a relatively new Pratt & Whitney afterburning turbojet, designated JT4A-25 by

JF-3, also known as 54-0112, the only JF-105B-2RE, flew in a modestly spectacular markings scheme during its heyday at Republic

the company and J75-P-5 by the Air Force. It could deliver a maximum static thrust of 23,500 pounds at sea level, burning JP-4 fuel at the rate of 776 pounds per minute. Without the afterburner, its static thrust ratings were 15,500 pounds (military power) and 13,700 pounds (normal power). Specific fuel consumptions, measured in pounds of fuel per pound of thrust per hour, were 1·98 for maximum thrust, 0·80 for military and 0·77 for normal.

The F-105 fire-control system – which also included equipment for nuclear weapons delivery – was the General Electric MA-8. It was an integrated assembly of GE equipment: an E-34 ranging radar, an E-50 gyro-computing sight system, an E-30 toss-bomb computer and a T-145 weapons system for the special stores.

Among the aircraft's 'new and novel features', the specification listed the bomb bay, which was 190 inches long and 32 inches wide and deep. It could carry, and eject, either one Mk 7 special store, as modified by Republic, or one USAF 'Bluff Shape', another

configuration for a nuclear weapon. Other new and novel features included the combination aileron and spoiler system and a variable-area ejector used in conjunction with a converging engine nozzle.

Specification ES-350 described the AP-71, or RF-105, and pointed out that its new and novel feature was a pair of M-39A1 20mm cannon installed in external blisters in a removable installation.

Laurence K. Loftin Jr, a brilliant and influential engineer then working at the Langley Memorial Aeronautical Laboratory of the National Advisory Committee for Aeronautics, recalled that the Republic designers had done their homework. The F-105, he said, incorporated all the features that had been found, up to that time, to be desirable for an aircraft designed to fly in the transonic and supersonic range. Its wings and tail surfaces were swept at 45 degrees; the wing was thin, tapering from 5·5 percent thickness ratio at the root to 3·7 percent at the tip. It used trailing-edge Fowler flaps and leading-edge flaps to increase the maximum lift

ABOVE
NASA's 1/22-scale model of the F-105B final configuration.
The rear fuselage shows where area-rule bulges were added

LEFT
Sunlight sharply defines the Thunderchief's shape. The
waisted fuselage, the aggressive inlets, the compliant wings

---

coefficient. Roll control was achieved with short-span
outboard ailerons assisted by upper-surface spoilers to
reduce the adverse wing twist associated with large
aileron deflections. The all-moving horizontal tail –
called the stabilator – was chosen for increased
effectiveness in the transonic and supersonic regimes, and
was mounted in the low position to aid in preventing
pitch-up. The high wing loading and the low wing area
favoured low drag at supersonic speed.

In spite of all those features, the two YF-105A models
were capable only of flight investigations at subsonic
speeds. The design required much more thrust,
preferably from an afterburning engine that could
produce the power required over a broader speed
spectrum. It needed new engine air inlets to assist the
increased intake airflow and the shock waves generated in

supersonic flight. Perhaps most of all it needed a major
reduction in transonic drag, to penetrate well into the
supersonic cruise range. Some concern also had been
voiced at Republic about the possibiity of tail flutter in
high-speed flight. Remember that back in the first post-
war decade, supersonic flight was not routine, was not
clearly understood and was capable of sudden surprises to
pilots and engineers alike.

The Air Force had requested NACA to begin a test
program in support of the Republic design as early as
1954, a year before the first flight of the YF-105A.
During the years that followed, engineers at Langley –
after October 1958, the Langley Research Center of the
National Aeronautics and Space Administration (NASA)
– were to test and analyse all the basic production models
of the F-105. Models were studied in the subsonic,
transonic, and supersonic speed range in a variety of wind
tunnels. Dynamic models were 'flown' in free-spinning
tests in a spin tunnel. The NACA/NASA studies
concentrated on stability and control characteristics,
details in the design of the F-105's distinctive engine air
inlet and the general aerodynamic performance of the
aircraft.

'It would be fair,' said M. Leroy Spearman, a NASA engineer who worked on some of those tests, 'to say that the F-105 design was dramatically influenced by the NACA/NASA studies.' Unarguably the most dramatic of the several influences was the application of the area rule to the design of the F-105. The area rule, almost always called the 'Coke bottle effect' by the uninitiated, was the brainchild of Richard T. Whitcomb, later to win the Collier Trophy for his contribution to the advancement of flight. His novel concept for drag reduction at transonic speeds had been verified by him and by other NACA researchers during December 1952, three months after Republic's receipt of its first contract for the F-105.

Whitcomb says that the early wind-tunnel data on the F-105A led to the same general answers as did the tests on the first model of Convair's F-102 Delta Dagger interceptor. The F-105A would not be able to meet its guaranteed performance and could not comfortably exceed Mach 1 by any substantial margin. Whitcomb suggested the addition of carefully contoured and

ABOVE
Detail of the air inlet for the Pratt & Whitney J75 of this F-105B, now in retirement at Long Island's Cradle of Aviation Museum. The plate parallel to the fuselage separates the low-velocity boundary-layer air from the inlet flow

RIGHT
Among the last tests performed in NACA's 19-ft pressure tunnel at the Langley Aeronautical Laboratory were those made during 1954 on this quarter-scale model of the F-105

positioned bulges to the fuselage of the F-105, thus gaining a better and smoother distribution of the cross-section of the F-105 in accordance with the basic principle of the area rule. That, he knew, would reduce the transonic drag.

Telling the designer of an elegant aircraft to put bulges on it is a sure way to gain an abrupt refusal. Kartveli fought to keep things as they had been designed; one Republic associate remembered that the great man had resisted the substitution of a bubble canopy for the framed cockpit of the P-47 Thunderbolt and had said that

ABOVE
The mockup of the F-105C shows just what an elegant two-seat aircraft it might have been

LEFT
Showing all its dramatic features this early F-105B, photographed at Edwards AFB, was engaged in the flight test program

it looked like a pickle on a lovely airplane. Underneath, however, Kartveli was also a realist and he agreed to wind-tunnel tests of a model modified to reflect Whitcomb's proposals.

NACA by then had made a number of test runs on the original configuration of the YF 105A. Among other problems was one that surfaced during tests in the 4-foot supersonic pressure tunnel. Most early supersonic aeroplane designs shared a common failing of directional stability deficiencies at the angles of attack associated with normal manoeuvring. The standard remedy was to increase the vertical tail area; NACA recommended a 32 percent increase in that surface and the further addition of a ventral fin, to supply stability at very high angles of attack where the normal flow over the vertical tail might be partially blanketed by the downwash from the wing.

Spearman listed a series of schemes that were also tested, but not adopted, to improve the directional stability. They included horizontal strakes on the forward fuselage, cruciform strakes on the afterbody, twin ventral fins, twin 45-degree dorsal fins and folding and retractable ventral fins.

NACA had a 1/22-scale model of the YF-105A which had been tested in several wind tunnels and they modified it to reflect not only Whitcomb's area rule theories, but also to incorporate some other aerodynamic suggestions. The fuselage was bulged, aft of the wing, additional vertical tail surface was added, to improve stability and control at supersonic speed, and the nose was lengthened because the Air Force wanted a radar there which didn't match the existing lines of the A model. The subsonic inlet was changed to a supersonic type – and there's a separate story to be related regarding this.

31

This belly landing is most likely the one made by Henry Beaird on the maiden flight of the first F-105B on 26 May 1956

Kartveli sent an observer to NACA, and the tests began. The results showed that the F-105 modified shape would slide easily through the transonic zone and well into the supersonic, as promised in the design which had originally been submitted to the USAF. When Alexander Kartveli saw those results, and after studying the model, he agreed that maybe the wasp-waisted airplane didn't look too bad after all. However, he had the last word; he would only accept a bulge reduced to about 80 percent of the recommended size. That, said Dick Whitcomb, is basically how the F-105B lines evolved from those of the YF-105A prototype.

The total amount of wind-tunnel time spent on the developmental testing of the F-105 was approximately 5,000 hours, according to one NASA engineer. All the subsonic testing was done in the Langley 19-foot tunnel, using a 1/4-scale model of the aircraft. The 1/22-scale model was used for transonic tests in the 8-foot transonic pressure tunnel and for supersonic tests in the 4 × 4-foot supersonic pressure tunnel and the Langley Unitary Plan wind tunnel. Other studies were done in the 7 × 10-foot tunnel and the free-spinning tunnel.

The development of the odd-shaped inlets for the F-105B and subsequent models – and for no other aircraft since – is a story that is probably like that of the origins of the AP-63 design itself. There must have been a number of sequential or parallel studies proceeding with a single goal in mind. Republic veterans remember that the basic shape was developed in-house, by an engineer named Nucci. Said one, 'We were working on the XF-103 then, and it had a belly inlet that sloped forward; and one day we came up with the thought that we might split the inlet and put half of it on each wing of the F-105'.

Former NACA engineers credit part of the inlet development and design to the late Antonio Ferri, then at NACA, who solved some of its inherent problems, but whoever and whatever influenced their design, the inlets finally evolved to a highly efficient type. The fact that they worked (and those on North American Aviation's YF-107A developed a frightening and destructive duct 'buzz' – 'More like cannon firing about a foot behind my head,' said former NAA engineering test pilot Albert W. Blackburn –) was one of the reasons that the YF-107A was dropped from consideration as a back-up programme to the F-105.

The F-105 design team chose a variable air inlet system, universally referred to as the VAI. Its purpose was to match the engine inlet airflow to the requirements for maximum engine efficiency over the very wide and demanding speed range from zero to Mach 2. It used a set of movable contoured plugs in the inlet itself, whose adjustment changed the capture, or cross-sectional area, of the inlet. Additionally, there was a set of air-bleed doors on the fuselage. Plugs and doors were operated through hydraulic actuators. A set of auxiliary air inlet doors led to the wheel wells and was intended to be operated only when the wheels were extended.

One characteristic of a turbojet engine is that its thrust

Although labelled F-105D, this is the nose mockup of the RF-105, with its slab-sided sections for oblique camera positions and hatches on the underside for vertical cameras

is proportional to the total pressure at the inlet, once a set of operating conditions has been established. That total pressure is the sum of the static pressure – the ambient barometric pressure at a given altitude – and the dynamic pressure – a function of air density and the square of the velocity. Inlets are designed to obtain the highest possible fraction of the dynamic pressure through efficient recovery, so that the total pressure, and therefore the thrust, will be a maximum. That's not an easy task, because the amount of air the engine wants varies with flight speed.

There are two alternatives. One is to use a fixed geometry for the inlets and accept the best compromise available, with some deterioration of performance. The other is to use variable geometry inlets, with plugs and bleed doors to vary the capture area to take in the optimum amount of air for each speed. The latter route is

complex, difficult and very necessary to achieve the best in performance. It was selected for the F-105.

In automatic operation and during take-off, subsonic acceleration, climb or cruise, the plugs remained fully aft, leaving the inlets unobstructed so that they could swallow the high volume of air needed under those lower-speed conditions. At transonic speed, the VAI system was activated, and from then on, was controlled by information from the aircraft's central air data computer. Up to about Mach 1·5, the bleed doors could operate, depending on temperature and air-speed combinations, but above Mach 1·5, the bleed doors were opened, regardless of temperature, to let out any excess air that might itself act as a choking agent in the inlet ducts. The plugs moved forward, according to a schedule determined by the Mach number and the computer. By the time the F-105 has accelerated to Mach 2, the plugs were fully forward.

NACA did accomplish a major test program on the inlet, obtaining useful data over a range of angles of attack at supersonic Mach numbers of 1·41, 1·81 and 2·01. They also found that the model inlet had a relatively small stable operating range, hinting at possible in-flight problems with the real thing, but Republic engineers were able assure their NACA counterparts that no such problem existed with the full-scale inlets, proving that model tests don't necessarily provide all the answers.

There were two other features of the F-105 design that were, and remain, unusual or unique. One of them was the layout of the four petal speed brakes installed on the aft fuselage. The second was the inlet in the base of the vertical fin, used to capture air to cool the after end of the fuselage. It's worth noting here that the original air supply to the rear didn't supply enough ventilation and, after some incidents, additional air scoops were added to the fuselage sides.

So the aerodynamic formula for the F-105 evolved. It began with a good basic shape, but it needed modifications and additions to achieve its guaranteed

The third F-105B, carrying a mixed bomb load and a centerline tank on a test mission, is probably at Eglin AFB, site of the Air Force Armament Center

FH-102 begins its take-off roll down the runway at Edwards AFB. The first few aircraft were built with the small rear-view windows aft of the main canopy; they were deleted on later aircraft

performance. To those modifications, both NACA and the Republic engineers made major contributions. There is enough credit for both.

Early in the game, Republic engineers who were planning the flight-test program had begun to worry, as engineers in that position always do, about the effects of possible flutter of the wing or tail surfaces. The requirement for thin wings and tail surfaces meant that classical flutter theory, based on subsonic aerodynamics, was probably useless to predict the possibility and extent of the flutter problem. One early approach, used in the F-105 program, was to flight-test small surfaces, dynamically similar to those of the full-scale F-105, attached to a typical fuselage shape propelled by solid-fuel rockets. These tests tended to give yes or no answers, but were not suitable for finding out where and when the flutter phenomenon began.

Langley had a 26-inch transonic blow-down tunnel operating then and it seemed to be the ideal research tool for some flutter studies. On 18 October 1954, two models of the all-moving horizontal tail of the F-105A were delivered to Langley for testing. An answer was not long in coming. On 27 December, one of the models tore apart in a flutter test that simulated the normal operating speed range of the F-105A. A few days later, the second followed the same destructive course. It was obvious that the horizontal tail of the F-105 had a serious flutter problem.

By empirical means the tail design was strengthened and the F-105A was cleared for flight, but, as Larry Loftin, then in charge of those flutter tests, remembers, 'The exact nature of the problem was never clearly identified and the solution represented something of a brute-force approach.'

At the same time, there was concern about the vertical tail. Tests that had been made during late September 1955, showed that a buzz developed, serious enough in one case to cause the loss of the model rudder. Investigation showed that the rudder itself reacted in a mode of torsional vibration which eventually amplified and destroyed that control surface. Viscous dampers at the hinge were required to cure the fault.

In 1956 and 1957, further flutter tests were made at NACA on the proposed tail design of the F-105B, planned for higher speeds – and therefore higher loads – and with a different style of connecting yoke between the two halves of the all-moving horizontal tail. That design was also cleared for flight.

This vital study of tail surface flutter undoubtedly prevented serious problems – and possibly fatal accidents – resulting from flutter in flight. The study was under the control of NACA, but Republic and Dynamic Devices Inc, the Dayton, Ohio, firm that designed and built the models, were equal partners.

In the months following the first flight of the YF-105A (22 October 1955), Republic's engineering department was working under pressure, making changes in old drawings and starting the lines for new drawings. The original handful of designers had been augmented until, at the time of first flight, more than 300 engineers had been assigned to the F-105 program, under Project Engineer Sidney R. Huey. By the time a heavy design schedule began on the B model, the company had about 370 engineers on the project. It's often forgotten that the Republic designers at that time were working in New York City, in a suite of offices and drafting-room space rented in the Dun & Bradstreet Building. They had to be transferred nearer the production line.

More than 90 percent of the engineering personnel that were involved with the program at that point elected to make the move to Farmingdale. The company provided

ABOVE RIGHT
The fourth and last of the F-105B-1RE block (54-0103) takes-off from Farmingdale, Long Island, on a test flight

RIGHT
The RF-105 was cancelled, and the planned prototypes were given the unusual designations of JF-1, -2 and -3 by the company. Serial 54-0105 was the first of this trio of test aircraft

The first JF-105B-1RE brakes to a stop on the runway at Republic, completing its first flight. Flaps are full down, the split petal drag brakes are wide open, the drag chute is deployed. This angle emphasises the 'all-fuselage-no-wing' appearance of the F-105

some assistance in finding housing and arranging car pools. One Friday afternoon, everyone checked out of the New York design office at the end of the day. On the following Monday morning they reported for work in a renovated office space above the main factory floor of the Farmingdale plant. Their desks, drafting tables, libraries, files, blueprint machines, water coolers and pencil sharpeners had been moved and were in place, ready to be used immediately.

Among other engineering efforts during early 1956 was the development of the F-105C, a two-seat version of the B model, designed to a specification issued by Training Command. Its tandem seats were under an elegant extended bubble canopy. The mock-up was approved and in April 1956, Republic received the go-ahead to build an initial evaluation batch of five aircraft.

The first F-105B (54-0100) made its maiden flight at Edwards AFB on 26 May 1956. Republic test pilot Henry Beaird had completed his air checks and was returning to Edwards; he went through each item of his pre-landing check list, selected gear down and expected a normal response. Instead, he was annoyed to find that

RIGHT
This would have been the second RF-105A, but instead it was destined, only, to fly test missions. The second JF-105B-1RE (54-0108) leaving on a test flight from Farmingdale, Republic's home base

BELOW
A demonstration of in-flight probe-and-drogue system refuelling. Notice the angle of the tanks with respect to the fuselage thrust line of the second YF-105A (54-0099); needing all the lift it can get, it is trimmed at a high angle of attack. Tank drag was minimized by aligning them to the anticipated airstream. The receiver is the third F-105B-1RE (54-0102). The two profiles show clearly the difference in vertical tail area between the two prototype A and B models

only the main landing gear had extended. He was getting two green indicator lights and one red; the nose wheel was still in the well. Beaird tried the usual remedies and none worked. Up came the main gear for the last time and Beaird landed the F-105B on to the dry lake bed after making a fast and flat approach. The aeroplane received only minor and repairable damage from the landing, but the operator of the wrecking crane, called out to move the dead bird from the runway, managed to drop the aircraft about one foot. It was enough to crack the fuselage at Station 285, necessitating more than minor repairs when the plane got back to the workshops.

Fighters need appropriate names and the F-105 was nearing maturity without one. Naturally, Republic wanted to maintain the 'Thunder _ _ _ _ _' series and applied on 19 June 1956, to the Air Force for approval of Thunderchief. The USAF approved that selection on 25 July and in August the naming ceremony took place.

The three RF-105 models on order and in work were cancelled in July, to be completed in a new identity and designated JF-105B, (the J prefix indicated they were temporarily classified as special test aircraft). Without camera installations in the modified nose, they had volume and weight capacity for test equipment and instrumentation. All three were lent by the Air Force to Republic upon their completion and were assigned to flight-test duties. Republic pilot Lindell ('Lin') Hendrix flew the first JF on 18 July 1957 and for the next four years, the three JF aircraft were used in flight evaluations of flutter, the autopilot system, of a wide variety of external stores and of ways to jettison both internal and external weapons and droppable fuel tanks, to name just a few examples.

Hendrix had experienced an unusual in-flight emergency early that year. He was in the landing pattern after a successful check flight with the second F-105B (serial number 54-0101) on 30 January 1957, when his

F·105D
ALL WEATHER
MOCK UP

U.S. AIR

The mockup of the all-weather F-105D, the aircraft the USAF really wanted, shows the crammed nose section loaded with black boxes. The sign is in the cockpit area

warning lights showed that the main gear was still in the wells. He got permission to try for a belly landing and set up a flat final approach at 190 knots. The plane touched the runway, and the magnesium ventral fin flared, but there was no other problem. After the scraping sounds ceased, Hendrix unstrapped and climbed out to await the arrival of the wreckers. As he walked away from the grounded aircraft, the main wheels slowly dropped from the wells. It was a puzzler; the embarrassed Hendrix had tried all the accepted tricks to drop those wheels while in the air and it wasn't until some time later, after everybody had thought and analysed and speculated about the incident, that the real reason was discovered.

The auxiliary engine air intakes in the wheel well had somehow been opened while the wheels were still retracted; enough suction was developed in the well to keep the wheels in place against gravity and the natural forces of extension. An interlock was designed rapidly and installed in the auxiliary inlet system, to keep it from being actuated when the wheels were retracted and that problem was solved.

Hendrix noted later that, since three of the first four F-105s had made belly landings, quantities of belly-landing repair kits were put into the pipeline as spare parts, in accordance with the standard practices of weapon systems procurement. However, after the intial

experience of a high frequency of unforeseen belly landings, the rate subsequently dropped to almost nil and a large number of repair kits continued to gather dust.

Another kind of embarrassing incident occurred in May 1957, as if to underline some of the sillier aspects of trying to maintain security on a 30,000-pound assembly of metal that flew noisily from place to place. The well known and respected French magazine *Aviation,* in its issue of 1 May 1957, published a major article on the F-105. Its author deduced a large number of facts, previously undisclosed because of USAF security restrictions. He did it simply by analysing a single published, retouched photograph, the only one released to that date.

Republic was furious, not at the revelation, but because the company itself had been refused permission to release a few more pictures or facts on the aircraft for publicity purposes. The USAF had held firm in its refusal. The revealing article in *Aviation* was cited by Republic as yet another reason for letting some new pictures be published. Finally, the service relented. The F-105B

One of the last in the F-105B-20RE production block, 57-5836 wears the tail badge of the Tactical Air Command. Shown probably on one of the many armament test missions required to prove the Thunderchief as a weapons system

would be displayed – and photographs could be made public – during an air show scheduled for 28 July at Andrews AFB, Maryland.

Planning for the new D model began about mid 1957; it was clear that what the Air Force really wanted was an all-weather supersonic fighter-bomber and the F-105B was only a good performer in sunshine. The five F-105Cs became casualties of the new emphasis on the D. Their contract was terminated in October, when Republic received a new order for 20 F-105Ds and eight F-105Es. The latter were two-seat models otherwise identical to the single-seat D.

In November 1957, the Air Force published a new and completely revised GOR 49, which called for substantial changes in the F-105 design. It required the fighter-bomber to carry the new TX-43 nuclear store and to be equipped with an AN/APN-105 Doppler radar all-weather navigation system, new cockpit instrumentation incorporating the use of tape display instruments where practicable and a target-towing system. These requirements were to be incorporated into the D design.

Under the Cook-Craigie plan, Republic had built an initial batch of 15 aircraft, with the expectation that all of them would be devoted to test programs. Two were the YF-105As, three were JF-105Bs (two of those, plus four F-105B aircraft, having been built as the -1RE block), there was a single JF-105B-2RE, five F-105B-5RE and a single F-105B-6RE.

By early 1958, 11 different F-105s were in various test programs. The ninth aircraft (serial 54-0107) was flying out of Eielson AFB, Alaska on Arctic operational tests. It had previously completed laboratory ground tests in the gigantic climatic hangar at Eglin AFB, Florida, where its engine had been run and its systems operated at temperatures down to −65°F.

The three JF aircraft were flying at Farmingdale doing systems components testing. Another was assigned to train pilots to fly the new bird. Four were operating at the Air Force Flight Test Center (AFFTC) in follow-on assessments by USAF pilots. One of these, too, was at Eglin AFB evaluating the MA-8 fire-control systems and armament at the Air Proving Ground Center (APGC). One, a non-flying example, was undergoing static-load tests at Wright Air Development Center (WADC), Wright-Patterson AFB, Ohio.

The next three successive production aircraft (serials 54-0109 and 54-0110, both -5RE models, and 54-0111,

the solitary -6RE) were to be assigned to a program jointly conducted by Republic, TAC, Air Research and Development Command (ARDC) and APGC to simulate combat conditions.

By 15 April, 643 flight tests had been completed, including 163 by 20 different USAF pilots (among whom was Captain Melburn Apt, later to be killed in the crash of the Bell X-2, and Lieutenant-Colonel Frank K. Everest Jr, who had won the Harmon Trophy the year before for his pioneering experimental flights in rocket-powered aircraft, including both the X-1 series and the X-2). Seven Republic pilots flew the remaining 480 test flights. During March, the program had logged a total of 65 flights, including 41 at AFFTC, nine at APPGC, seven at Eielson and eight at Farmingdale. Among other accomplishments was a seven-minute turn-round time on

LEFT
A production F-105B on the ramp at Farmingdale prior to its first flight

The third F-105B-5RE, marked with the red tail and wingtips of Arctic-based aircraft, is on the ramp at Eielson AFB, Alaska, for cold-weather operational tests in early 1958

a special test, a remarkably low figure for a new aircraft and still an outstanding performance in 1983.

By now, Republic's engineering department numbered close to 1,300 men and women, and there were about 10,000 drawings on file that detailed the shape of every production piece and part. The public relations people were working on a release to be issued when the first F-105B was formally accepted by TAC, an event expected to take place late in May. The release was full of what writers call 'Gee-Whiz numbers', series of facts that publicists hope will pep up a routine story.

The release pointed out that one-third of the cost of the F-105 was accounted for by its installed electronics system, that there were more than 65,000 individual items in every F-105 and that it took 26 times as much engineering effort, measured in hours, as did the World War II P-47 Thunderbolt built by Republic. Altogether, said the release, more than 5 million engineering man-hours had gone into the F-105 by mid April 1958.

The first production F-105B was accepted at the plant on 27 May 1958, about three years late. And the Air Force, although praising the F-105B, still really wanted the all-weather F-105D.

3

Partly Cloudly, Some Rain

With the planned IOC date now three years behind schedule, Tactical Air Command (TAC) was eager to get the F-105 into service with minimal further delay. Normally, there would have been a transition period between factory deliveries and operational squadron assignments, the time being devoted to a variety of test programs conducted by different non-operational agencies within the Air Force. TAC decided that the Command could not afford any further schedule slippages, and elected to conduct Category II testing (the user command's first full evaluation of performance) with one of the units due to receive the fighter. In that way, the argument went, the time-lag could be minimized.

On 1 May 1958, the 335th Fighter (Day) Squadron was assigned to Eglin AFB, Florida, less its personnel and equipment – a routine method of unit transfer – and Detachment 1 of the squadron was organized with its operating location at Eglin instead of at its long-time permanent station, Seymour Johnson AFB, North Carolina. The 335th was one of four squadrons of the 4th Fighter (Day) Wing, proud descendant of the famed Eagle Squadrons of World War II and the first TAC combat-ready wing scheduled to be re-equipped with the F-105.

Detachment 1 became part of a joint test staff with members from the Weapon Systems Project Office, Air Materiel Command, Air Force Flight Test Center, Air Proving Ground Command, Wright Air Development Center and Republic. Project officer was Lt-Col Robert R. Scott, commander of the 335th TFS.

The test program was defined by TAC and the Air Research and Development Command. Central data collection was used to eliminate duplication of effort. As maintenance and logistical data accumulated, it was

Two New Jersey Air National Guard F-105Bs, 141 TFS, 108 TFW slide into formation with a tanker on a 1979 refuelling mission

incorporated into squadron procedures, again with the aim of shortening the time gap between testing and operations.

In August, the first production F-105B was delivered to the recently redesignated 335th Tactical Fighter Squadron, and the transition to operational status began. With production slippages, mandatory modifications in systems and components and special tests of sub-systems that were new to the airplane and the USAF, it took until mid 1959 – ten months – to supply that first squadron with 18 Thunderchiefs and another year until the 4th Tactical Fighter Wing was fully equipped. Ready or not – and it wasn't, then – the F-105 had been declared officially operational by the Air Force in January 1959.

The in-commission rates of the F-105B were appalling during the first few months. Less than one-quarter of the aircraft were flyable at any one time, due to several principal causes. A major, large-scale engine retrofit program was one. The first two production blocks of the B models off the line – nine of the B-10 and 18 of the B-15

sub-types – had been powered by the Pratt & Whitney J75-P-5 engine. In the B-20 and subsequent models, the engine was the J75-P-19, an upgraded power plant with another 1,000 pounds of badly needed thrust. Production P-19 engines had to be retrofitted in the Block 10 and 15 aircraft. Additionally, the autopilot, the central air data computer and the General Electric MA-8 fire-control system were unreliable and there was a continuing lack of spare parts and components. Maintenance requirements, complicated by frequent failures of materiel, were as high as 150 hours for each flight hour.

Factory production of the F-105B was running into many difficulties. Republic's original production schedule, WA58-1, which called for 65 B models to be produced between July 1958 and November 1959, could not be met. Republic blamed the slippages on the large number of mandatory changes that were required by the USAF. Neither were two successive and revised production schedules, WA58-3 and WA58-4, met. The latter called for two aircraft to be delivered in October

1958, a three-month slippage. They were; but then F-105B-10RE (57-5777), the second production B model, was lost in Long Island Sound during an acceptance flight test. In November, Republic told the Air Force that no B models would be available and asked for a further schedule revision. Additionally, the company took the unprecedented step of stopping the production line, in order to allow some time for critical parts to arrive and mandatory changes to be made, for aircraft already on the line. The Air Force, its patience tried to the extreme by this fourth failure to meet production schedules, sent an investigating team to the factory.

Republic argued, and accurately so, that the primary problem was one of unfamiliarity with the demands of a weapons system contract; neither the company nor the Air Force had much experience along those lines. The Cook-Craigie plan was criticized, because the early aircraft being delivered were not required to have all the tactical capabilities of later versions. Solving their

RIGHT
Thunderchief FH-111, the Indian head on the vertical tail is out of place, it should be on the fuselage side under the cockpit

BELOW
Shown here is the correct position, below the cockpit, of the Indian head of the 335th TFS. The tail stripe bears the TAC insignia; also a matching nose stripe. This pair 57-5797 and 57-5787 are from the F-105B-15RE production block

problems wouldn't be much help in the future. And the Air Force was criticized for specifying a low rate of production and frequent block and model changes.

The Air Force team report was critical of the production stoppage; it indicated that the company had lost control. It also suggested some other actions, including better reporting of problems to Republic management. Re-starting of the production line was scheduled for mid-December and that ended the crisis.

Meanwhile, there was another kind of crisis facing the company. In November 1958, the USAF made an Operations Safety Survey of the flight operations at Republic at the request of the Air Materiel Command. Its recommendations were severe. Operations of USAF jet aircraft from Farmingdale were to be discontinued as soon as possible. A lack of aircraft to fly kept Republic pilots from maintaining jet proficiency in night and instrument flying. For the same reason, their VFR daylight flying was at a level that would only provide minimal, or even doubtful, proficiency. High-time test pilots had averaged just above nine hours per month during 1958, and low-time pilots were logging only three hours each month.

The fact was that a delivered F-105B was a wonderful aircraft. It flew well, handled well, performed well. It was honest in the traffic pattern, had an effective drag chute for braking (although non-operation of the drag chute was the most-common malfunction during the early operations) and was relatively insensitive to cross-winds. It showed no tendency to pitch up in high-speed manoeuvres, a serious failing of the competitive McDonnell F-101 Voodoo, among others. When the bomb bay doors were opened, there was no trim change. It could drop its internal stores without encountering any buffeting or stability loss and with no effect on manoeuvres. It was solidy stable out to the far corners of its flight envelope, even with stability augmentation switched off. Its guns showed consistent accuracy; 80 percent of the rounds fired during the test program hit within an 8mm circle (a dispersion of eight parts in 1,000).

It was, in short, a remarkable aircraft – and for the moment, TAC was moderately satisfied. The 4th Tactical Fighter Wing (TFW) began its work-up to full strength and both Republic and the Air Force continued to study improvement programs.

The first non-testing operational unit to receive the B models was the 334th Tactical Fighter Squadron (TFS), 4th TFW. The initial allotment of four arrived in a single flight on 16 June 1959, 10 months after the 335th had begun its pioneering test program with the first models off the Republic line. At that time, the Wing included many young captains with 1,500 to 2,000 hours of logged flying time, who – to qualify for F-105 conversion – had to have at least 200 of those hours in Century-series fighters (since the 4th TFW was equipped with North American F-100C Super Sabres before it traded them for the Thunderchiefs, the acquisition of 200 hours of time in a Century type was no difficult task).

Making the conversion from the F-100C to the F-105B required about 75 hours of flying and a 16-day ground

ABOVE
Six F-105B-20REs, from the 334th TFS of the 4th TFW, based at Seymour Johnson AFB, North Carolina, yet to be decorated with the eagles that identify the 334th and refer to the origins of the 4th TFW. The 4th Fighter Group (later 4th TFW) was formed 12 August 1942, its air echelon from 71, 121 and 133 Squadrons, the three Eagle Squadrons of the Royal Air Force

RIGHT
Republic's production line is headed by the 18th of 66 F-105D-5REs built. The line is typical of the times

school. Since there were then no available two-seater F-105s, pilots went solo on their first flight, after a thorough study of the handbook and time spent sitting in the cockpit to become familiar with the switches and instrumentation. After learning the basics of F-105B flight, they completed a series of ten simulated combat missions to bridge the gap between flying an aircraft and fighting with it. Even then, the squadron was far from being a fighting entity.

The chronological story of the 4th TFW summarizes

LEFT
The 25th F-105D, 58-1173, from production block 5RE, on a
practice bombing mission

BELOW
The 'Chiefs' have made the transition from the B model to the
D; FH-719, 59-1719, a D-5RE with the TAC badge on the tail,
the Chief below the cockpit, and a nose stripe

complex. The exercise began on 24 July 1961 and lasted
several weeks.

For almost a year, the squadron flew routine missions,
building up time and experience in the F-105B. Then, on
20 June 1962, all B and D models were grounded for
inspection and modifications as necessary. The flight
controls had to be re-rigged, hydraulic lines which were
suspected of chafing – a major and potentially dangerous
problem on the F-105B – had to be inspected and
replaced if necessary, and all modifications that had been
approved to that date had to be incorporated.

Project 'Look Alike', as the fix and modification
program was named, was expected to take a few weeks
after the scheduled work under its Phase I had begun on

the continuing training that the 334th experienced after
receiving their new aircraft. In mid July 1960, a year after
their first F-105Bs had arrived, the unit deployed with its
aircraft to Williams AFB, Arizona, for the Category III
tests of the armament system. Those tests, normally done
by one of the Air Force's non-operational agencies, had
been delayed until modifications of the MA-8 fire-control
system could be completed. Continued malfunctions of
that system and a lack of repair parts added to the delay,
and Category III was finally completed in mid August.

With the conventional armament system evaluated, the
next stage was training and qualification on what the
USAF euphemistically calls 'special weapons'. The
course in nuclear weapon delivery techniques and effects
was given at Eglin AFB and the 334th deployed there in
the late autumn, completing the tour on 15 December.

The next major training schedule took the 334th to
Nellis AFB, Nevada, for another course in the delivery of
weapons, both nuclear and conventional, and in gunnery,
using the instrumented ranges at that vast desert

18 July. Like almost everything else in the F-105
experience, Look Alike took longer than expected. It
became a two-year effort, eventually costing more than 50
million Dollars. Teams of technicians from the Mobile
Air Materiel Area (MOAMA) of Air Force Logistics
Command (AFLC), augmented by Republic field service
representatives and factory technicians, assisted the
mechanics of the 4th – and other units, that by then were
equipping with the more-advanced F-105D model – to
complete the requirements of Look Alike's first phase. It
took until 30 November to finish all of the work on the 60
F-105Bs at Seymour Johnson AFB; there was a enforced
interruption to cope with an international crisis.

On 18 October, TAC OPLANS 312, 314 and 316 went
into effect, alerting the 4th TFW to the threat of a
conflict. On 21 October, the Wing was ordered to deploy
all combat-ready crews and aircraft to McCoy AFB,
Florida. The Cuban missile crisis had erupted, and the
country was girding itself for what was believed to be an
almost-inevitable war, possibly involving the use of

nuclear weapons. Many of the F-105s were undergoing the Look Alike modification and were unavailable for flying, let alone fighting. Combat crews were recalled and 20 F-105s – including some D models – had to be borrowed, with their aircrews, from the 4520th Combat Crew Training Wing at Nellis AFB, where the Thunderchief training program for instructor pilots on both models was underway.

The 4th TFW began a one-hour alert status at 4.00 am on 22 October, with its war-loaded aircraft dispersed at McCoy. That afternoon, as the Cubans and their Russian patron, Nikita Khrushchev, held firm, the one-hour alert was cut to 15 minutes. It was as close to the brink as the nation had edged in some years and the flight crews were betting they'd be airborne and headed south within 24 hours.

In the event it was five days before they were airborne, but in a different role. Armed for an air-superiority mission, patrols of F-105s from the 4th TFW flew

ABOVE
Rocket pods empty, a pair of F-105Ds proceed back to base after a tactical training mission. Gas deposits around the gun port of FH-745 are evidence that the Vulcan cannon has also been fired

RIGHT
You can almost count the rivets holding the FH-750 together. Every marking, skin joint, and material change shows in this detailed rera three-quarter view

routinely over the southern Florida peninsula, ready to intercept the Ilyushin bombers or MiG fighters whose arrival would signal an air attack on the United States. On 29 November the 4th packed its gear into the fleet of Thunderchiefs and headed back to Seymour Johnson; the crisis was over.

Early in 1963, the 334th flew south again, this time to MacDill AFB on the Gulf coast of Florida. There the unit qualified its pilots in gunnery, with live firings at towed air targets and at floating rafts. It was a pleasant way to spend the first couple of weeks in any January, especially after the tense weeks of the past autumn.

The 4th was then, and still is, a fighter unit with a NATO commitment; its 335th and 336th squadrons are now dual-based, assigned to a West German location as well as to Seymour Johnson, and deploy for long periods on a regular basis. In the last days of April 1963, the 334th packed its bags and readied its aircraft for an overseas deployment. Crews rehearsed their over-water routines, paying special attention to their emergency equipment. They checked their vaccination records and brought them up-to-date with whatever new immunities they needed. A few took paperback English-Spanish

dictionaries when they headed for their aircraft, because the 334th was flying to Moron Air Base, in Spain, on an operation designated Fox Able 147. It was the first rotation of the F-105 to NATO and, until they were relieved on station by the 336th TFS, a sister squadron in the 4th TFW, the pilots of the 334th flew missions with their allies in a new environment. They were back home by 13 August.

Little time was allowed to settle in, however. There were routine missions during the pleasant autumn months of North Carolina, and then the word came through that the wing would be trading in its F-105Bs for the new and improved all-weather F-105D. The re-equipment began on 26 January 1963, completing a period of about 4½ years which had been both frustrating and fulfilling.

Massive retaliation and the F-105

The administration of President Dwight D. Eisenhower, who took office in 1953, had developed a national security doctrine based on the concept of massive retaliation. Simply put, the doctrine warned that

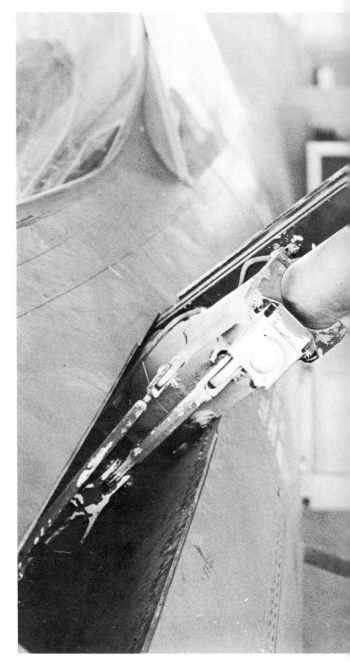

aggressors could expect a return strike equating to the total destruction of their country by nuclear weapons. It was a concept that rested on the comforting assumption that the United States would have a monopoly in nuclear weapons for a substantial period of time; it was also a concept that ignored completely what might have to be done in the event of something less than total war.

The doctrine of massive retaliation was reflected in defense budgets; massive amounts of dollars went to buy delivery systems for nuclear weapons and, in those days, Strategic Air Command (SAC) was the prime beneficiary. SAC had bombers by the hundred and was busy carving out control of future long-range missiles to bring all the methods of nuclear weapons delivery under its jurisdiction.

TAC fought for its funding by arguing that classic tactical airpower missions included deep interdiction strikes that could utilize nuclear weapons. Tactical nuclear warheads were beginning to become available and TAC saw a way to make nuclear bombers out of its fighters. The F-100 led the way; it had been designed as a day fighter, for the air-superiority role, but the realities of the budget battles quickly eliminated that role and the F-100 became a fighter-bomber with a nuclear capability.

The F-105 suddenly took on a new glamor. It had long range, blistering speed and the ability to fly safely at low altitude and high speed. Further, it had a bomb bay big enough to carry tactical nuclear weapons. TAC decided to go with the Thunderchief as a way of securing its place in the strategy of massive retaliation.

ABOVE
The probe for the in-flight refuelling system, housed in a recess on the port forward upper fuselage. The pilot needed to see it and the drogue for contact. Shown a F-105B at Long Island's Cradle of Aviation Museum

ABOVE LEFT
The 783 designation on the radar reflector refers to F-105B-10RE, 57-5783, formerly of the New Jersey Air National Guard and now on display in the Cradle of Aviation Museum. Both the nose and the main gear of the F-105 look surprisingly light and lean for the job

ABOVE RIGHT
The starboard main landing gear of old 783, ground lock pin and red warning flag in place

There were some opposing internal Air Force viewpoints that had to be countered somehow. General Lauris Norstad, a long-time bomber general, was then Supreme Allied Commander in Europe. As such, he controlled the operations of all tactical aircraft on the scene. Norstad said in 1958 that those aircraft were sitting ducks on the ground and that they all ought to be replaced with medium-range ballistic missiles. That, of course, would have wiped out TAC's nuclear functions almost entirely; there was then little likelihood of a threat in any other corner of the world.

In 1959, TAC's new commander General Frank F. Everest, just back from a two-year tour as commander of United States Air Forces in Europe (USAFE) under Norstad, took an indirect swipe at the F-105. It needed too much concrete, he said, and what NATO really needed was a fighter that could use a 3,000-foot-long unprepared field.

Everest took command of TAC at the beginning of an intensive effort to increase the limited-war capability of the Command. It was an effort that called for force modernization, increases in force strength and the ability to deploy those forces world-wide to meet any crisis. One result was an immediate evaluation of every existing TAC weapons system, carried out by the Command with supporting efforts from Headquarters, Air Materiel Command, and Air Research and Development Command.

TAC operations officers liked the F-105, but TAC upper echelons wanted a cheaper aircraft than the F-105D, whose cost figures were beginning to indicate higher levels than anticipated. Pentagon studies indicated that McDonnell's F-101 Voodoo could be bought less expensively. Its twin-engine, two-seat layout had caught the eye of Pacific Air Forces commanders and they were pushing the F-101 as ideal for their kind of long-range, over-water operations. Costs can be deceptive; the unit price of the F-101 was indeed lower than the F-105D, at that stage. But there was a big difference in capabilities between the two aircraft, and to give the F-101 the same combat abilities as the F-105D would have required a major and expensive modification program.

General Everest wanted to be able to get TAC aircraft off the ground and into the air fast. His stated goal was that 65 percent of the force should be airborne 15 minutes after the alert. His objection to the length of runway required for the F-105 stemmed in part from this alert-to-airborne goal. In fact, that short a response time was unavailable with any of the TAC units, let alone the F-105 squadrons. The only immediate solution was the ZEL system, a wild ride out of a hardened shelter on a rocket-boosted fighter. And not all TAC's aircraft could ride the fiery blast. The F-101's pitch-up characteristics, well known by then, worked against its launching by the ZEL scheme. North American's F-100 had been tested that way, successfully, and both the Lockheed F-104 Starfighter and the Republic F-105 were adaptable to ZEL.

The ZEL concept did not go much further than the early F-100 tests. Instead, TAC and the USAF immediately began studies to improve the F-105, to define a successor, to rethink the mission. A series of new design proposals came out of the Republic engineering department: a new, upgraded J75 engine; ways to enhance the potential of the F-105 to make it capable of accurate attacks in zero-zero weather; additional electronics; new navigation and guidance systems; extra weaponry; more fuel.

This F-105B, 57-5782, is surrounded with everything needed to go operational. Bombs, rockets, ammo, cranes, a Sidewinder missile, pilot and technicians

It was also probably no coincidence that, at about the same time, the Air Force planned and carried out a successful assault on the world speed record for a 100-kilometre closed course. The logical pilot for the attempt was Brigadier General Joseph H. Moore, commander of the 4th TFW. Preparations for the record run (code-named Project 'Fast Wind') included a series of preliminary flight tests conducted by Moore and by Major Charles W. Barnett, commander of the 4th TFW's 334th TFS. Republic's 'Rusty Roth' was brought in as an adviser, and played a unique role in the final record flight.

The course, historically flown around pylons at low level, was to be flown instead at 38,000 feet and on a circular path of 9·9-mile radius. One lap equalled 100 kilometres (62·14 miles). Course markers were a dozen 4×4in concrete slabs embedded in the dry lake surface at Edwards AFB.

The standard aircraft instruments were essentially useless for such a flight. Their accuracy, reliability and

time lag made them unsuitable for precision flying. The only available alternative was to fly the course on indications from a sensitive g-meter fitted in the F-105B. Ground radars and tracking cameras would confirm the accuracy of the flight path, and furnish additional information to the pilot – and that's where Roth came in. His job was to assist Moore by calling off the g-meter readings required to maintain the accuracy of the flight path.

On 11 December 1959, Moore climbed into his F-105B, took off and headed for the initial altitude of 38,000 feet. He stabilized the aircraft in straight and level flight, aiming for the 'gate', a point tangential to the circular path, and roared into it at over 1,400mph. On the ground, Roth called off g-readings, guiding Moore in a nearly constant 3·5g-turn.

At about 20 miles per minute, Moore held the F-105B in a sustained turn, fighting the strain of multiplied g loads on his body and senses. It was over in about three minutes; Moore had broken the existing record by a substantial margin notching up an average speed of 1,216·48 mph.

With the attendant publicity and other strategies, TAC held off further damage to the program for a while longer. Then, President John F. Kennedy was inaugurated, in January 1961. Kennedy's Secretary of Defense, Robert Strange McNamara, was a man whose name today evokes expressions of absolute contempt from virtually all the

aircrews who survived the air war in south-east Asia. McNamara had a mandate from Kennedy to strengthen the forces of conventional warfare. Massive retaliation was dead; the Russians had long since broken the nuclear monopoly, and a guerrilla war was raging in south-east Asia.

McNamara established task forces to study a number of defense questions, including what to do about tactical aircraft. The F-105 was one of the subjects; at that time, it did not have sufficient provisions for hauling a significant underwing load of iron bombs. In April 1961, McNamara said that the earlier F-105s needed modifications, specifically a more powerful engine and underwing pylons for conventional ordnance. However, in November, he cancelled the F-105 program, preferring instead the Navy's McDonnell F-4 Phantom II, at that stage a more versatile aircraft. As part of the continuing effort to find an F-105 replacement, the Pentagon had issued SOR (Specific Operational Requirements) 183 in mid July 1960. It described a fighter that could take off

LEFT
Four camouflaged F-105Bs from the New Jersey ANG formate on a tanker

BELOW CENTRE
F-105B-20RE, 57-5823, served with the Air Force Reserve 466th TFS, part of the 419th TFW, at Hill AFB, Utah. Reserve and Guard units are noted for the excellent condition of their aircraft. This F-105B carries low-visibility markings, also the so-called 'wrap-around' camouflage scheme, with the darker upper and lower surface colors

BELOW
In June 1969, when McConnell AFB was the training centre for Thud drivers, this F-105B-20RE, 57-5835, was operated by the 4519th Combat Crew Training Squadron of the 23rd TFW. Pilot was Col. Hartinger, who is now Commanding General, NORAD and ADCOM

from a 3,000-foot unprepared field, fly at Mach 2·5, reach 60,000 feet, carry a nuclear payload internally and operate under all weather conditions. It was to have a variable-sweep wing. It was to replace the F-105 in 1966. It was, of course, the infamous TFX specification, destined to become McNamara's Waterloo.

Robert F. Coulam, in his fascinating study of the TFX (*Illusions of Choice,* Princeton University Press, 1977), points out that its requirements '... essentially defined a supersonic low-level mission, the same as the basic

mission of the F-105. McNamara's only indication that he had learned from the F-105 design and mission concept was his stipulation that the TFX be capable of carrying 10,000 pounds of ordnance.'

In all, only 75 B models were built by Republic. Ten were, in effect, the lead aircraft for testing under the Cook-Craigie plan; the remaining 65 – less those lost from attrition and accidents – were the inventory to equip the under-equipped 4th TFW and, later, the units at Nellis AFB and McGuire AFB, New Jersey.

4
Local Thunderstorms

I t's important to remember that few things in aviation, particularly in the high-technology areas of military aviation, happen overnight. There is a long period of extrapolation and evolution, of gestation and hesitation, of one step forward and two steps backward, before significant changes occur. And so it was with the development of the F-105. Tracing its life cycle is difficult; it moves backwards and forwards in time, influenced by events and the state of technology.

In May 1957, the Air Force concluded that it was again time to try to develop an all-weather attack aircraft. This is a periodic exercise that the USAF experiences; it's an even bet that today, somewhere in the Pentagon, some officer is concluding that it's about time the USAF had a new all-weather fighter-bomber. In May 1957, it seemed as if the technology existed, and that it could be applied to a production aircraft as one way of accomplishing two goals. First, and at worst, it would provide a few test-bed aircraft for further development, should the system be not what was expected. Second, if the system did not work well, it could upgrade existing aircraft at a lower cost than developing and producing an entirely new type.

Republic was asked to submit a proposal for the conversion of the F-105B to an advanced all-weather single-seat attack aircraft. The C designation had been used for a short-lived two-seater, and so the next Thunderchief model in the series would be the F-105D.

Planning for the F-105D Thunderchief had begun in mid 1957. The fair-weather F-105B fighter was then still two years from full squadron service, but even that early, it was clear to the Air Force that the F-105 needed additional navigational and attack systems to enable its pilot to operate in adverse weather conditions. That meant major improvements and additions to the avionics system, to take advantage of the latest technology. The

FH-412 an F-105F on a test flight, over the waters of Long Island Sound

Air Force also specified more power, to help counter the propensity of the Thunderchief to put on weight. Three significant changes finally differentiated the D model from the earlier B: The powerplant, the avionics, and the instruments.

The F-105 had been designed around the high-thrust Pratt & Whitney J75 engine. The B model was powered by the -19 version, which developed 24,500 pounds of thrust with the afterburner in use. The D was to have the J75-P-19W, the additional suffix representing an engine that had a water injection system for a further thrust increase on top of that brought by afterburning.

The P&W J75 family were examples of the new two-spool engine geometry which used concentric shafts to allow turbine and compressor operation at each one's optimum rotational speed. The axial-flow compressor had 15 stages; immediately downstream was an eight-unit can-annular combustor, followed by a split, three-stage turbine. The compressor was divided into an eight-stage, low pressure compressor, driven by the second and third turbine stages, and a seven-stage high pressure compressor, driven by the first stage turbine. The water injection system discharged through a spray ring into the compressor inlet, cooling the charge air and increasing the mass flow through the engine. Since thrust is proportional to mass flow through the engine, an increase in mass flow yields an increase in thrust.

With maximum afterburning and water injection, the -19W developed 26,500 pounds of static thrust at sea-level conditions. During each second, its inlet gulped 262 pounds of air – a volume equal to about three average-sized rooms – at that rating, and it burned fuel at the rate of 972 pounds per minute. With afterburner only in use the corresponding thrust was 24,500 pounds. Military rating was 16,100 pounds, with a fuel burn rate reduced to 220 pounds per minute. The figures for maximum continuous operation were 14,300 pounds and 188 pounds, respectively.

The second major difference lay in the AN/ASG-19 Thunderstick fire-control system (official terminology

dies hard; the ASG-19 was really a bombing and
navigational system, but fighters must have fire-control
systems). The Thunderstick set-up was designed to give
the F-105D pilot either a visual or a blind delivery option,
for nuclear or conventional stores, and air-to-air and air-
to-ground attack modes, using either guns or missiles.
The ASG-19 included the NASARR R-14A radar,
developed by the Autonetics Division of North American
Aviation. The R-14A represented a considerable
improvement over the limited E-34 ranging radar that
was part of the MA-8 fire-control system of the B models.
The Autonetics equipment had search and ranging
functions available in either an air-to-air or an air-to-
ground mode. Further, it was lightweight and operated in
the X-band of frequencies, for improved detection.
AN/APN-105 Doppler radar had been installed in an
earlier modification to the B models and was to be kept
initially on the D.

The third difference was in the type and layout of the
instruments. The YF-105A and the F-105B models had
the standard circular-display instruments, common to
aircraft since they were first adapted from steam and
water gauges in the early days of flying, but the D
introduced a new style – actually the concept dated back
almost to World War I – of vertical-tape instruments, in
which a series of vertical bars indicated key information
that was supplemented by additional data on the faces.
These instruments were on the panel in a T-formation
which was much easier to use for bad-weather flying.

The concept behind that installation was to present
flight information by means of movable lines related to
fixed reference lines. The movable lines presented
variable information that the pilot managed and matched
to the readings of reference values, generally preset by the
pilot. For certain operations, such as an instrument
landing approach, the movable lines were set

LEFT
FH-719 over the Atlantic coastline in the markings of the 335th TFS, 4th TFW. A late production F-105D-5RE, service number 91719, serial 59-1719

BELOW
With live bombs loaded on the centreline, outboard and inboard wing pylons, FH-173 gets airborne. The aircraft is a D-5RE, serial number 58-1173

automatically by the on-board avionics to display heading and attitude information to the pilot. He kept the movable lines aligned with the fixed references, and thereby followed the commands of his avionics systems.

Four new instruments made up the F-105D integrated instrument system. At the top center of the 'T' was the attitude director indicator (ADI), which displayed roll and pitch attitudes also rate of turn and slip, as well as computing bank steering information, glide-slope displacement for instrument landings, and both bank and pitch information to intercept and maintain position on the glide slope and localizer beams. Directly below the ADI was the horizontal situation indicator (HSI), that showed the pilot the magnetic heading, the bearing, the command heading, course information, displacement from the course, to-from indication from a desired TACAN (Tactical Air Navigation) and the distance to the TACAN station, a target or the destination. A quick scan vertically of the ADI and HSI gave the pilot the equivalent of a vertical reference and a downward view.

To the left of the ADI was the airspeed Mach indicator (AMI), which presented safe speed warnings, vertical g loads, the true Mach number, and the calibrated airspeed.

On the right of the ADI was the altitude vertical velocity indicator (AVVI); it displayed vertical velocity (equivalent to the rate of climb), the pressure altitude and the altitudes of the cabin and the target. A horizontal scan was equivalent to having a forward view with a horizontal reference.

Augmenting the integrated instrument display were other advanced avionics systems. The automatic pilot was the AF/A42G-8 automatic flight control system, with three modes of operation. It could augment aircraft stability, relieve the pilot of some work-load, or take over completely for fully automatic flight. In the last of these modes, it could make automatic instrument landing approaches and automatic toss-bomb runs. The all-attitude compass system provided pitch, roll and azimuth information and served as the directional reference for the navigation and flight-attitude displays. Its data was fed to 11 different systems or indicators in the F-105.

An AN/ASQ-37 CIN (communications, identification, navigation) system included the AN/ARC-70 UHF command set, for voice transmission over long line-of-sight distances, the AN/ARA-48 DF group, to find the relative bearing to any 225 to 400 mc transmitter within range, the AN/ARN-61 instrument landing system with glide-slope, localizer, marker beacon, and visual-aural indications, the AN/ARN-62 TACAN, with range and bearing information, the AN/APX-27 identification radar system, to provide identification data to an IFF interrogation, and the AN/APN-131 Doppler navigator, to compute solutions for great-circle courses anywhere on the globe.

ABOVE
First of the Ds, 58-1146 taxis along the runway at Republic's
Farmingdale, Long Island, plant

LEFT
Thunderchief FH-343 takes on fuel during an overwater
exercise

The AN/ASG-19 fire-control system was named
Thunderstick by Republic. It was an integrated group
that computed and directed a wide variety of armament
functions:

visual dive, visual/blind level-approach bomb attacks and all-
attitude releases of special or conventional free-fall weapons;
visual or blind level-approach bomb attacks, with level
release of special or conventional retarded weapons;
visual/blind level-approach bombing attacks with
anticipation of computer solutions with all-attitude releases
of special or free-fall weapons;
visual air-to-surface attacks with gun or rockets;
visual air-to-air attacks with gun or rockets;
visual or blind air-to-air pursuit attacks with Sidewinder
missiles;
blind tracking for air-to-air gun, rocket and missile attacks;
blind air-to-air search for gun, rocket and missile attacks;
navigation aid with ground, terrain maps and terrain
avoidance.

In mid December 1957, and again in April 1958, the
cockpit mock-up of the D model – the key component,
and the major visible difference from the F-105B aircraft
– was given a thorough inspection and critical
examination by the Air Force Mockup Board. The Board
passed it and the F-105D was officially given a
production go-ahead.

Externally, the F-105D was in most respects a
dimensional duplicate of the B. There were some design
details that were different, because of the new
installations, but basically it seemed like the same
Thunderchief airframe. Republic said otherwise,
however, in asking the Air Force for new production
schedules: the D weighed more, required new main
landing gear, wheels and brakes; the new engine would
require some design changes in the aft fuselage and its
increased airflow would mean some ducting changes as
well. Putting it all together, said Republic, it looks as if it
will take 214 work-days to build each aircraft, instead of
the 144 that it is now taking to build the F-105B.

There were two basic structural concepts that made the
F-105 airframe different from most of the others in the
industry and that contributed to its great strength and its
later-proven ability to take the punishment of war. One
was a dividend from the spoils of an earlier conflict.
German production experts in World War II proved that
the use of large forgings at points of high stress created a
lighter, cheaper airframe without sacrificing strength and

so, on the basis of those experiences, the Air Force sponsored the post-war development of huge presses to produce the large and complex forgings required for contemporary airframes. Republic was an early pioneer of that technique and used many such structures in the F-105.

The second new concept was applied to the outer shell. The industry was then covering its aircraft with sheet aluminium alloy of constant thickness, resulting in a structure that was heavier than it needed to be, but Republic pioneered the use of machine milled skins, shaving them down to a varying thickness for the optimum distribution of strength and weight. It was a more expensive method of production, but it led to lighter structures.

The wing of the F-105 seemed small, even taking account of the reasons for its minimal area. It measured 385 square feet, which meant that wing loadings for maximum weight take-offs began at about 120 lb per square foot and went up from there as time went on. High wing loadings do nothing for altitude performance, and as those who flew it found out, the F-105 was no high-altitude craft. However, those wing loadings were ideal for operating low down and fast. The sweep-back angle of the wing, measured at the quarter-chord point according to the classical aerodynamic convention, was 45 degrees, ten more than the long-established norm of the previous generation of fighters.

Aerofoils were NACA low-drag types, with a 65A-005.5 section at the wing root and a 65A-003.7 section at the tip. The last two figures indicated the thickness ratios: 5·5 percent and 3·7 percent respectively. By the standards of the day, that was a thin wing, again best-suited to low-level, high-speed flight.

The wing was set high on the fuselage so that the horizontal, all-movable 'slab' tail could be set low. That was the layout recommended by NACA to avoid longitudinal stability problems that had been endemic in some of the F-105's sister Century fighters. Putting the wing up high meant that the landing gear would be longer, and therefore heavier, than it would be with a typical low-winged layout of the day, but that was regarded as a small price to pay for the better and safer handling qualities.

The wing had both leading-edge and trailing-edge flaps. The former were full-span, and had a 20-degree maximum deflection. The latter were partial-span Fowler-type flaps, with a 34·5-degree maximum deflection. For landing and take-off, both flaps were used at full deflection. For cruising and manoeuvring at

ABOVE LEFT
On 18 September 1963, the USAF's Tactical Air Command had at least 36 flyable F-105s, and this picture proves it

LEFT
In Western Europe it rains a lot, here at Hahn AB in Germany a few F-105Ds put their new lacquer finish to the test. In the foreground is 60-0430, an F-105D-10RE from the 36th Tactical Fighter Wing, based at Bitburg

subsonic speeds, only the leading edge flaps were lowered, by about 8 degrees.

The lateral control system was a dual one, with small outboard ailerons and a five-segment spoiler inboard, the ailerons being locked out at high speeds. The low-set horizontal tail operated as a piece; it had no separate elevators. All the controls were powered and artificial feel was used to give pilot feedback. Ailerons and stabilizer were operated by hydraulic actuators in tandem (later to prove a bad design choice), each powered by primary 1 and primary 2 hydraulic systems. There was also an emergency system, with power supplied by a ram-air turbine that extended automatically into the slipstream.

Historically, wheel brakes have never been powerful enough to stop hurtling, heavy aircraft in a semi-emergency landing condition, so the F-105 had a 20-foot-diameter drag parachute, and it was used routinely for all landings, to reduce the landing roll, and to minimize brake wear. If all else failed, the Thunderchief also had a tail-hook, housed in the ventral fin, to pick up any of the runway over-run systems (BAK-6 water squeezer, BAK-9 brake system, BAK-12 tape system, or MA-1A chain barrier).

Republic designers developed the novel petal speed brakes as a combined brake and two-position ejector nozzle for the engine. In afterburner mode, the petals automatically opened by 9 degrees to produce a larger ejector nozzle. With landing gear extended, only the horizontal petals could be fully opened and with the gear up all four could be fully opened.

All the fuel in the F-105 was in the fuselage, in three tanks: forward (376 US gals), main (257 US gals) and aft (502 US gals), for a total of 1,135 US gals internally. There were provisions to carry a pair of wing-mounted tanks (900 US gals total), a belly tank (390 US gals) replacing the weapon. Including 25 US gallons trapped in fuel lines, the maximum fuel load possible was 3,100 US gals or 20,150 pounds.

The engine drew fuel from the internal tanks; the external ones were used in managed sequence to replenish the internal tanks. They were designed, and initially built, with an explosion-detection-and-suppression system, but the Air Force later deleted it to save weight and cost (putting similar protection in later, as a result of combat experience, was a costly modification). Refuelling was done at a single point, on the ground. Airborne, the F-105 could refuel at tankers equipped with the probe-and-drogue system, using a retractable probe mounted on the left side of the fuselage ahead of the cockpit. Late model F-105D-31RE aircraft were also equipped with the now-standard USAF refuelling receptacle, for contacts with boom-equipped tankers.

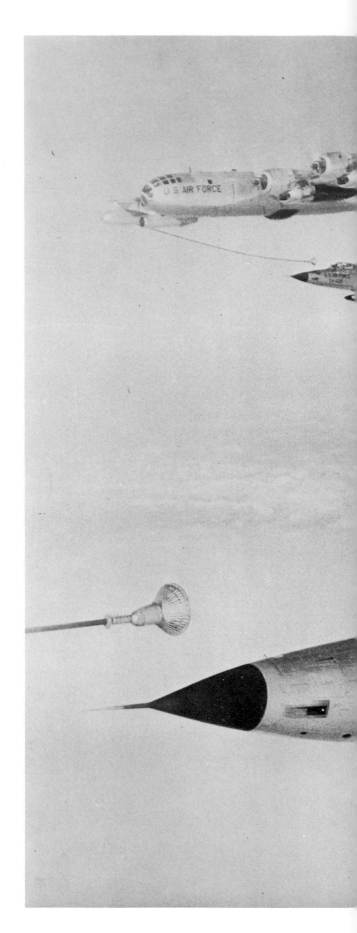

FH-469 about to contact the refuelling drogue trailing from a Boeing KB-50 tanker. In the background two F-105s have already made contact. The aircraft are from the 36th TFW, Bitburg and are probably on ferry flight as part of Project Look Alike. Date 28 August 1963

As a final touch, there were provisions for a thermal radiation screen in the cockpit, a two-piece affair that would shield the pilot after he released the special store.

On 9 June 1959, the first F-105D-1RE, serial number 58-1146, made its first flight, with Hendrix at the controls. It was, at that point, one month ahead of schedule. As a flying machine, the F-105D was as close to perfect as anything the pilots had ever evaluated. It was universally praised, then and later, because of its superb handling qualities, its stability, its feel in the air. Pilots called it a Cadillac. The problem was that the Air Force, and particularly Tactical Air Command, couldn't afford Cadillacs. What they really wanted were Chevrolets that felt like, looked like and drove like Cadillacs – an impossible dream!

The first thing to do in such a situation, as far as the Air Force is concerned, is to initiate a study to determine if and where money can be saved. A committee is formed to study what can be removed from the aircraft without compromising its ability to perform its intended combat missions. That was done. The Air Force convened a Configuration Board that included officers from United States Air Forces in Europe (USAFE) and Pacific Air

Forces (PACAF), the using commands that would depend on the F-105 for a major portion of their tactical strength. TAC and Air Force Headquarters were represented, as well. The Board considered the roles of the F-105, its systems, and its capabilities and performance.

The Board recommended that the F-105 be lightened and cheapened by removing the M-61 cannon, the explosion-suppression system for the fuel tanks, the APS-92 radar warning receiver, the ALE-2 chaff dispenser, the ALQ-31 jammer and a few other backup and optional systems. A parallel cost study designated 'Wire Brush' expected savings of this stripping would amount to about $105,000 for each aircraft.

It should be noted that the officers from USAFE and PACAF argued strongly that the cannon should be kept. They were outvoted – and also outranked – by the other Board members, who believed that the cannon was not serving any effective purpose.

Sixteen F-105 fuselage nose sections illustrate the scale of the production line

It also should be noted that, some time later, minds were changed and the Air Force retained the cannon in the F-105. It was just as well, because eventually accounted for the greatest number of MiG-17 kills by F-105 pilots.

Proving the Thud in Service

Like its predecessor, the F-105B, the D model went into Category II flight testing with the 335th TFS at Eglin AFB. Problems with the J75 engine delayed the start of those tests from May until December 1960, but the testing of the airframe during the F-105B Category II tests and of the engine during Category I on the D model, meant that some of the work could be eliminated and other tasks reduced in scope.

The test program at Eglin evaluated the things that were different on the D: the navigation system, the fire-

control system and the new instrument layout and functions. The evaluation pilots were pleased and when it came to the flight characteristics, always one of the Thud's stronger points, they wrote a laudatory report.

'The F-105D differed little from the F-105B with respect to aircraft handling and flight characteristics.... As compared to the other Century-series aircraft flown by the transition pilots, the overall handling characteristics of the F-105D, as with the F-105B, were considered to be superior. The stability of the aircraft about all axes was the most dominant factor. As in the F-105B aircraft, favorable aspects included excellent manoeuverability and high g performance characteristics at all altitudes; good lateral or pitch control at minimum approach speeds; superior formation flight characteristics; and impressive in-flight acceleration and deceleration, using afterburner and speed brakes.... Transition from subsonic to supersonic flight is smooth and, from a stability standpoint, practically unnoticeable. The excellent power response, coupled with the overall stability, makes the F-105D, like the F-105B, a relatively good aircraft with which to accomplish all phases of transition training' – Report APGC-TDR-62-12, *Joint AFSC/TAC*.

Thunderchief FH-467, 60-0467, a D-10 block aircraft at the final assembly point of the production line

Category II System Development Test and Evaluation of the F-105D, February 1962.

One example of the Thunderchief performance was demonstrated dramatically soon after the Category II testing began. Lieutenant Colonel Paul Hoza, commander of the 335th TFS, flew an F-105D non-stop from Eglin to Nellis AFB, Nevada on 10 July 1961. The 1,520-mile run was made at altitudes between 500 and 1,000 feet above the terrain, took in a simulated nuclear weapon delivery and was flown blind all the way – and that included a leg through mountain passes after a refuelling stage above the Texas 'panhandle'.

One of the controversial performance items was the Thud's maximum gliding range. Most people would assume that the F-105 had the glide performance of an anvil, but from 40,000 feet, it could reach a point almost 60 miles distant. That glide ratio, distance to altitude, worked out at 7.75 for the F-105D. The operator's handbook for a Cessna 150, the ubiquitous light plane with which just about every novice pilot has practised engine failures and gliding, shows a glide ratio of 8.8. That's only about a 14 percent improvement on the F-105.

Meantime, pilots who were to fly the Thud were learning the ropes with the 4520th Combat Crew Training Wing, at Nellis AFB. The first class of 21 student pilots began training early in 1961, on a 61-day course designed to familiarize them with the system and

flight characteristics of the F-105D. They logged about 45 hours of flight time each during the course, with more than half of it spent on radar navigation and simulated combat missions. Only a small proportion – $5\frac{1}{2}$ hours – was spent on the conversion to F-105Ds from the F-100s they had been operating.

The first two F-105Ds went to Bitburg Air Base, Germany, on 12 May 1961, assigned to the 22nd TFS of the 36th TFW. They were followed by other D models in flights of four to six, until the 22nd TFS was at its authorized strength of 24 aircraft. Then the next group went to the 23rd TFS, and finally to the 53rd TFS, completing the wing re-equipping.

In October 1961, the 49th TFW moved to a second West German field, Spangdahlem AB, with its three squadrons of F-105s: the 7th, 8th and 9th TFS.

In those days, USAFE maintained an elaborate Weapons Center at Wheelus AB, near Tripoli, Libya. It was the training ground for the majority of the tactical fighter-bombers and interceptors. The first F-105 crews

RIGHT
Created from battle-damaged parts of several Thuds. This aircraft stands in the grounds of the Air Force Academy as a memorial to graduates who served in Vietnam

BELOW
SSgt William Scroggins and Sgt John Dean, 2951st Combat Logistic Support Squadron, are installing an upper wing skin over the landing gear bay on Thunderchief 482

Republic has begun to build the F-105E models, and here is the first one on the line. Basically, it was a stretched D with a single-piece bubble canopy covering the two cockpits

LEFT
The cockpit of an F-105D, taken at Hill AFB in June, 1983

deployed there from Bitburg on 16 July 1961 and began training in the delivery of nuclear weapons. It was a difficult course, the pilots averaging as many as four sorties per day with typical mission times of 1 hour 20 minutes. Only the 20-minute segment was over the range, practising the bombing. The rest of the flight was spent getting to and from the range, holding while awaiting clearance for the run-in and orbiting for rendezvous for the return flight.

Occasionally, the bombing training produced some extraordinary experiences for the F-105 pilots. Captain James S. Walbridge, from the 8th TFS, 49th TFW, had his test under pressure when the throttle on his F-105D jammed in full military power during his second dive-bombing target run on the Wheelus range. Walbridge was an 'old head', with more than 3,000 hours in jet fighters, and he drew on all his experience to solve the problem. The only technique available to control his

speed was the addition of drag. He extended the petal speed brakes, and began a series of high-*g* turns to load the aircraft and soak up its power. In that way, he was able to slow the F-105D below the limit speeds for flap and landing-gear extension. With them out and dragging and still making his high-*g* turns, Walbridge headed for the 11,000-foot runway at Wheelus.

He approached in a series of S-turns, still trying to bleed off as much speed as possible. About half a mile out from the threshold of the runway, he hauled the F-105D into a complete 360-degree turn at about 220mph and an altitude of 250 feet. While still turning, he cut off the fuel, rolled out of the turn, and glided the last half-mile to touch-down. His Thud was still indicating 220mph when it touched the runway; the normal touch-down speed was 190mph. The F-105D rolled and rolled and rolled, using up 9,500 feet of the Wheelus strip before the forces of friction finally won and the airplane stopped.

The average pilot required eight missions to qualify for nuclear weapons delivery and air-to-ground gunnery. Every two months or so, the crews would have to return to Wheelus to spend another two weeks honing their skills. About 10 percent of the wing strength could be found at Wheelus at any time, but they logged a major portion of the total Thud flying hours.

Look Alike for the F-105D

During mid 1962, the Ds entered the Look Alike
modification program, to bring all of them up to the
standards of the -25RE production block of aircraft. A
major part of the program provided for the quadrupling
of the F-105's capacity to carry externally mounted
750-pound iron bombs. Before the modification, the
plane's standard armament loads included one of four
750-pound bombs. After Look Alike, 16 could be carried
on multiple racks, for a bomb load of a nominal 6 tons
(actually, the 750-pound bomb weighed 823 pounds, so
16 of them weighed in at 13,168 pounds, or about 6·6
tons).

The modification program required, among other
work, the expensive process of opening the fuselage by
removing flush-riveted skin panels, so Look Alike
engineers and technicians took advantage of the
opportunity by installing guidance system components
for Bullpup missile launching, adding changes to the
refueling probe and the fuel system and installing a tail-
hook in the ventral fin assembly. It was at this time also
that the external finish was changed from raw unsealed
metal, with unfilled seams which had allowed water to
seep into the avionics systems, to aluminized lacquer,
which effectively sealed the seams and other minute
cracks and almost removed the chances of a repeat of the
water problems.

To give one example of the extent of the work required
under Look Alike, in addition to the major changes listed
above, consider the -10RE aircraft flown by the 36th
TFW at Bitburg. Those craft required 385 technical
order (TO) changes to bring them up to -15RE standards,
while the 49th, at Spangdahlem, flew a mix of -25RE and
-20RE Thuds, which needed a lesser number of TOs.

The aircraft were ferried to MOAMA by USAF pilots,
cycled through Look Alike at the depot and returned to
Bitburg after about one-month. The ferry flights,
conducted under the name of Project High Flight
strained the maintenance personnel of the 36th and 49th
TFW. It took about 4½ days to get an F-105D ready for
the flight back. They departed in flights of four, with two
spares on standby, for the 4,400-mile journey to
MOAMA. The trip lasted more than 10 hours and
included three air refuellings.

Development of the two-seat Thud

When the two-seat F-105E was cancelled in 1959, it
was predictable that a future need for a two-seat trainer
would certainly arise. Flying the F-105D, with its
complex weapon systems and its semi-automated
delivery, was a procedure that needed careful study and
monitored transition. It was possible to study; but there

Basically, an F was a stretched D. The vertical tail also had
increase height and chord, to compensate for the added area
ahead of the center of gravity. On the ramp at Republic is
FH-412, 62-4412, the first of the F series

was no way that an instructor could ride along with a student on his first check ride in the single-seat F-105D. So it came as no surprise to Republic that Secretary McNamara gave a go-ahead for the development of a two-seat F-105 in May 1962. There was a gap in training procedures; student pilots needed to be able to achieve proficiency in navigation and in the bombing systems in order to operate the F-105s with maximum efficiency, but there were no aircraft available that could be modified or adapted to the job at any reasonable cost. The company, having gone through the particular design exercise twice before, with the F-105C and E models, was thoroughly familiar with the task required.

The last 143 single-seat F-105D-31RE aircraft were, in effect, cancelled, and replaced by an equivalent number of two-seat models to be designated F-105F. The primary role for the new model was defined as exactly the same as that of the F-105D: tactical bombing. Its secondary tasks included the simulation of such missions for training purposes and the training of aircrew in the use of radar, instruments and other electronic equipment.

It was a relatively simple conversion. The fuselage was stretched by 31 inches ahead of the wing to provide the space for a second cockpit. Then, because the center of gravity had moved forwards, the aircraft needed additional vertical tail surface area for directional stability and that was provided by increasing both the chord and the vertical span of the fin and rudder assembly. The

larger tail would in turn produce increase tail loads, so some structural reinforcement was added in the aft and center fuselage sections. The landing gear mechanism was modified to increase the maximum retraction speed to 350 knots and the forward fuel cell was redesigned to match the same unit in the F-105D.

The second cockpit was equipped for a second pilot, although later events were to require the use of an electronic warfare officer to concentrate on operating some of the special systems, and to let the pilot devote his attention to flying the mission as required. Otherwise, the F was a D, with all its advantages and problems and with a weight increase of more than 3,000 pounds.

The F-105F-1RE (62-4412) came off the final assembly line on 23 May 1963 and first flew on 11 June 1963, 40 days ahead of schedule. Republic Aviation pilot, Carlton B. Ardery Jr, pushed the F-105F above Mach 1 on its first flight and reported that the new machine had no vices and was pretty similar to the D.

Within 6 months, the first production F model left the factory for delivery to the 4520th CCTW at Nellis AFB, the place where instructor pilots have been learning their specialized crafts for many years. Soon after that, one of the early Fs was sent to demonstrate its weapon systems to a series of high-level USAF commanders. The total demonstration was scheduled to require 88 flights, with an additional 11 allotted for functional checks or ferrying.

The F-105F completed 61 flights in 22 days spent at Langley and Andrews AFBs, logging 72hr 35min during low-level missions which included a supersonic dash and a simulated weapon delivery. Ferried across the Atlantic to Ramstein AB, it completed an additional 38 flights in 15 days, the only difference being that the supersonic dash was flown in a climb because of local noise restrictions. The weather during these latter demonstrations was typical of Europe: Ceilings down to 300 feet, visibility 1 mile and moderate to heavy rain. No missions were cancelled because of weather and no flight was aborted. The aircraft maintained an average turn-around time of 18 minutes between flights.

RIGHT
Left side of F-105F forward cockpit. (RAC B-12962 via Drendel)

BELOW RIGHT
Right side of the F-105F forward cockpit

BELOW
FH-332 is ready for a simulated tactical support mission during Goldfire I, a Strike Command exercise held in south western Missouri from 29 October to 11 November 1964. The exercise was planned to test USAF ground-support techniques that had been developed as part of Strike Command's tactical operations. This immaculate F-105F is a late production aircraft, serial 63-8332. Only 34 more were built before the line closed forever

Aerodynamic design requires strange things, like the two different angles of the auxiliary fuel tanks. The centerline tank nearly parallels the thrust line; the outboard pair is angled to minimize their drag at high angles of attack

A factory-fresh F-105F front panel in aircraft serial 62-4422. (RAC B-17268-5A)

The equipment behaved in exemplary fashion. During the 99 flights of the demonstration program, the radar showed a mean time between failures (MTBF) of 43hr 10min; the CIN system, 87hr 25min; Doppler radar, 58hr 15min; the autopilot, 87hr 25min.

Category I tests were well underway then, having begun soon after the first flight, and because of the similarity between the F-105F and the F-105D, there were fewer tasks to accomplish under the USAF's service testing program. Category I tests were completed in July 1964 and category II tests, which had begun earlier, were completed in August.

USAF evaluation pilots rated the F as ideal for radar and instrument training and for annual instrument checks. Its rear cockpit was a choice location for the Flight Examiner putting a pilot through a Stan/Eval check flight, or for instructor pilots (IP) teaching the finer points of attack tactics, but the restricted visibility, said to be like looking through a double-barrelled shotgun, limited the usefulness of the F in other instructional missions. The IP would be of little use at the back in join-up, air-combat manoeuvers, Dart target gunnery or any type of in-trail flying where it was desirable to keep a look-out forward. Perhaps worst of all, the IP in the rear seat had not nearly enough forward visibility to supervise the flare for landing.

The aft instrument panel was mounted 3 inches higher and 6 inches closer to the instructor than to the pilot and to make it easier to read its top was tilted toward the rear

seat by 9 degrees. The combination of dimensional and angular displacements gave the instructor an optical illusion that the climb was steeper than normal. 'Afterburner climbs are a thrill to behold,' said one Captain. It worked both ways: the normal approach, viewed from the rear seat, appeared to be abnormally low and dragging, as if the Thud were going to touch down short of the runway. For that reason, any landings made by instructors during TAC's testing program were consistently poor and not a single IP volunteered to fly the F-105F solo from the rear seat.

By December 1964, the last-ever Thunderchief was moving slowly down the production line, leaving an increasingly large gap behind it. The Air Force accepted it in January 1965 and the F-105 production program was finished.

The F-105F went on to win renown as the mount of daring Wild Weasel aircrews, who took on the SAM batteries in North Vietnam. Most of the production aircraft were converted for this, or for two other special missions: Commando Nail and Combat Martin (see Chapter 10). A few served as two-seat trainers, their original role, with each of the units that operated the Thud. Combat losses of the F-105F were especially, and disproportionately, heavy. Only a relative handful

Instrument panel, rear cockpit, F-105F

survived the war – three squadrons' worth – and of those, 48 were in the active Air Force inventory, flying as Wild Weasels. They were part of the batch of F models that had been further converted, during the war, to the F-105G configuration.

Service with the Fourth

The 4th TFW, which had been first to use the F-105B, kept those first production models until early in 1964, when the 334th and 336th TFS began conversion to the F-105D. Within two weeks, all F-105s were grounded; they were inspected, released for flight and grounded again on 14 May, staying on the ramp until mid July. However, by mid year, 1964, the 4th had become a full-strength, four-squadron, tactical fighter wing, with 96 F-105Ds flying out of Seymour Johnson AFB.

This was a short period of peace. On 27 August 1965, the 4th received its first camouflaged F-105D and the next day, one of its component squadrons, the 334th, deployed to south-east Asia from Homestead AFB, Florida, where it had been training in the special tactics of pop-up delivery. There, the pilots had learned how to approach the target at an altitude of under 100 feet and a speed of 500 knots. This was followed by a screeching

pull-up to 10,000 feet, a half-roll to the inverted position, a quick scan for the target, a pull-down and another half-roll to position the aircraft for the bomb release.

The 334th TFS deployed to Thailand with 18 F-105D Thunderchiefs. The pilots were checked out locally within four days and started flying combat missions. They stayed in south-east Asia for five months, completing 2,231 combat sorties. This was an average of 15 sorties per day, or an 82 percent availability rate – outstanding for a first time in a combat zone.

The 335th followed on 3 November, and the 333rd was sent, on permanent change of station (PCS), to PACAF on 4 December. The 335th returned on 8 December and the following February the 334th came home. On 21 March, both squadrons began operating as the replacement training unit (RTU), training F-105D pilots for the war. It was a 16-week course, with each student pilot spending 197 hours in classrooms learning about the Thud and its systems and logging 19 hours in the simulator. That was followed by 90 hours flying the aircraft itself. By October, rumours had reached the wing that it would convert to F-4Ds and that the Thuds and the RTU mission would be moved out. These proved true, and within a month all the Thuds had left and the 4th was making the transition to the Phantoms its pilots have flown ever since. The F-105D and F models had served the 4th TFW for only 34 months. The wing had been fully equipped for just 28 months and the Thuds were grounded for two of those.

5
Into the Eye of the Storm

Early in the year before serious design work started on the Republic's Army Proposal 63, President Truman's National Security Council postulated a domino theory for south-east Asia. Its Memorandum 64, of 27 February 1950, suggested that 'The neighbouring countries of Thailand and Burma could be expected to fall under Communist domination if Indochina were controlled by a Communist-dominated government. The balance of south-east Asia would then be in grave hazard.'

There had truly been a grave hazard to the balance of south-east Asia, but it reached back in time at least to World War I. Politicians have short memories, though, and an understanding of the major trends of history has never been their strong point. Now, there was an immediate hazard and money was appropriated to help the French in their guerrilla war. So, in the summer of 1950, the first orders were cut for USAF personnel to go to French Indochina, there to support national policy by maintaining war-weary Douglas C-47 transports, among other tasks.

The years went by and the war and the F-105 went their separate ways. Then it was 2 August 1964, and North Vietnamese torpedo boats attacked the Navy destroyer USS *Maddox* in the Gulf of Tonkin, a body of water lying between China's Hainan island and North Vietnam. Two nights later, *Maddox* and the USS *C. Turner Joy* signalled that they were under attack, again.

President Lyndon B. Johnson asked for extraordinary powers, and Congress passed the Gulf of Tonkin resolution on 7 August, abdicating its own war-making powers granted by the Constitution it had sworn to uphold. Johnson had the authority to commit forces to assist the government of South Vietnam and he chose to excercise it in part through the deployment of air power. Two Martin B-57 Canberra light bomber squadrons, out

During the time of the officially denied bomb shortage, Thuds went out to drop a load of only three 750 lb bombs each. This pair also is armed with rocket pods on the outboard pylons

of Clark AB in the Philippines, moved to Bien Hoa; F-100 Super Sabre and F-102 Delta Dagger squadrons arrived at Da Nang; and, says one official USAF historical reference, '. . . still other fighters moved into Thailand.'

The 'other fighters' were F-105Ds from the 18th Tactical Fighter Wing based on Okinawa. They were deployed to the Royal Thai Air Force Base, Korat on TDY (temporary duty) – eight of them were standing alert at Korat within a week of the Gulf of Tonkin incidents – and the crews prepared for their first mission briefings. The Thunderchief had gone to war.

Their first combat mission was scrambled during August. A flight of four F-105Ds from the 36th TFS roared out of Korat on a rescue combat air patrol (RESCAP) mission. When they reached the area in the Laotian Plaine des Jarres where an aircraft had been reported downed, they spotted an orbiting de Havilland Caribou from Air America. Questioned by radio, its pilot reported knowing nothing about any bail-out, but said he

was having trouble with anti-aircraft fire and asked the Thuds to knock it out for him.

It was somewhat irregular, as there was no forward air controller to mark the target, but the Thud pilots, one at a time, made strafing passes in the general area that the Caribou pilot suggested. On the second pass, the Communist battery opened fire, hitting an F-105 and doing considerable structural damage. Its pilot, First Lieutenant David Graben, stayed with the plane and it got him back to Korat safely, as countless 105s would also do later.

Early in 1965, there were approximately 150 F-105s in the Pacific Air Forces (PACAF) order of battle. Additional Thunderchiefs began to be released by the 36th and 49th TFWs in USAFE as their fighters were replaced by Phantoms. The USAFE birds were routed by way of the 23rd TFW at McConnell AFB, Kansas, then the replacement training unit for F-105 pilots destined for combat. The last of the USAFE Thuds departed from Europe in early 1967.

The F-105 bore the initial brunt of the war in strike missions against targets that were being selected thousands of miles away – and those missions were not long in coming as the war escalated.

The first major air campaign mounted against North Vietnam was named Rolling Thunder – an appropriate choice – because the major component of the strike forces sent north was the Thunderchief. The first mission of that air campaign was dispatched on 2 March 1965, briefed to strike the Xom Bong ammunition dump about 35 miles north of the demilitarized zone (DMZ). The force was mixed and included 44 F-105s, 40 F-100s, seven RF-101s, 20 B-57s and tanker support by Boeing KC-135s of Strategic Air Command. The F-105s were from PACAF units, the 12th and 67th TFS, home-based at Kadena AB, Okinawa, and deployed TDY to Thailand (in the USAF parlance, those aircraft and aircrew were PACAF assets, operating under local control for the strikes).

Rolling Thunder was a bombing campaign that was not a bombing campaign. It was limited in its scope, aimed more at producing the proper psychological responses in North and South Vietnam than at destroying physical assets on the ground. It was a poor second choice for the USAF, which in late 1964 had been one of the services recommending a 16-day saturation bombing campaign in south-east Asia to seize and maintain air superiority (eight years later, Linebacker II had a similar aim; by then, the defenses in the North were formidable and the price paid by the USAF was much higher than it would have been in 1964).

So day after day Rolling Thunder strikes were armed, briefed, dispatched and flown – and day after day, the Thuds went north, carrying their ridiculously small bomb loads, refuelling on the way up and on the way back

ABOVE
This late-model F-105D-31RE, 62-4364 carries a six M117 750 lb bombs on the centerline rack

RIGHT
On the boom and venting fuel, this Thud is equipped with a pair on ECM pods, one of each outboard pylon

and being shot at with every form of anti-aircraft weapon known to military science.

As the campaign matured, the units on TDY were replaced by two F-105 wings, permanently based in the theater. The 355th TFW and the 388th TFW were deployed from the United States to Korat. Their strength approximated 55 aircraft each, and out of that total of about 110, between 80 and 85 would be available for combat on any mission day.

The basic package – the Air Force spoke in units of packages of aircraft, of forces, of routes – was a strike force of 16 Thunderchiefs, composed of four elements of four planes each. These were the ordnance carriers. They were given fighter cover by two flights of four aircraft, one at the front and the other at the rear of the strike force. Five minutes ahead of everybody was a four-plane Wild Weasel flight and a second quartette of Wild Weasels trailed the formation to cover the withdrawal from the target area.

Four Douglas EB-66 Destroyer aircraft took positions in orbits near the outer limits of the restricted areas around Hanoi and Haiphong, both cities being off-limits to attacking aircraft. Two flew north-west of the cities, two south-west, at an altitude of about 25,000 feet. They were protected by flights of MiG combat air patrol (MIGCAP) aircraft, the mission of the twin-jet EB-66s being radar-jamming to decoy and confuse the enemy air defenses.

LEFT
'Daisy Mae' is from the 357th TFS, 355th TFW, and she's totin' what must be a centerline load of SUU-30B dispensers for anti-personnel bomblets, plus a pair of 500-pounders with fuse extenders. 'Daisy Mae' was the 27th D built; block D-5RE, serial 58-1172

BELOW LEFT
Loaded with 500/750-pounders, some with fuse extenders for above-ground detonation, on the centerline MER and outboard pylons, this Thud is from the 354th TFS, 355th TFW, Takhli. The strike camera is fitted under the nose; several ECM blade antennas protrude from the belly ahead of the small cooling scoop, and the tail-warning radar housing is clearly defined above the rudder

BELOW
'Big Sal', flown by Capt. John Hoffman on the way back from a bombing mission. Hoffman's aircraft is F-105D-15RE, 61-0086, from the 44th TFS, 355th TFW, based at Takhli

North Vietnam had built a strong defensive system before the first Rolling Thunder strikes headed north; now the enemy began to move additional units in, with more materiel being supplied by both Russia and China. Further, these weapons were mobile, not tied to fixed pads of concrete that could be found and bombed. The missiles, radars and anti-aircraft artillery were moved from place to place as the threat moved and were installed in small clearings near military objectives, but also very near – in some cases, on – civilian installations that were forbidden to be chosen as targets by the strike planners.

The Communists had never had much of an air force, but they began to strengthen and improve the capabilities of what they had. In the spring of 1965, their pilots began rehearsing interceptions plotted by GCI radar and coordinated by competent and experienced ground controllers.

Breakthrough to Downton

When the strike forces went 'downtown', the pilots' popular term for heading north to Hanoi, they had to penetrate the most concentrated system of integrated anti-aircraft defenses yet devised. It combined light, medium, and heavy anti-aircraft artillery (AAA), much of it radar directed, surface-to-air missiles (SAM) and MiG-17 and MiG-21 interceptors. One example, a 10-mile length of railway, illustrates the density of the flak. The line ran between Hanoi and China, and buffer zones and safety zones around both locations left only 10-mile stretch that was open to attack. The North Vietnamese jammed more than 1,100 AAA units along that track section – an average of one gun every 48 feet!

ABOVE
Rolling Thunder was an appropriate name for the bombing of North Vietnam. This mass drop by a dozen Thuds formating on a single pathfinding EB-66 released a tight pattern of approximately 100 bombs, probably 750 lb M117s

RIGHT
Four camouflaged Thuds roar out of the southwest towards targets in North Vietnam, loaded with 750-pounders on fuselage centerline and wing outboard pylons

The first losses to MiG-17s occurred on 4 April 1965 and the first loss to SAM on 24 July 1965; but when the final figures were evaluated, it was North Vietnameses gunners who had accounted for about two-thirds of USAF losses to enemy defenses. If the pilots flew low, the Triple A hit them; if high, the SAMs found them. So they penetrated the defenses at 4,500 feet, an altitude that was a compromise between the maximum reach of the AAA and the place where SAM began to work efficiently. F-105 pilots operating out of Thailand would take off as one of the two 16-Thud strike packages scheduled both morning and afternoon. Once airborne, and formed up, each package headed almost due north for the Laotian border, refuelling south of that border. The big KC-135As were in race-track orbit there, to support the strikes, the mission planner having arranged for them to be waiting at about 15,000 feet, because the loaded Thud could not struggle any higher.

The tankers never attracted the public attention they rated, but in the bars at the clubs, tanker crews seldom had to buy drinks. They'd been responsible for saving the lives of fighter pilots more than once, and pilots don't forget things like that.

On 5 July 1966, for example, four Thuds had been

This angle, better than any other, summarizes the reasons for the Thud's stellar performance: Low-drag area-ruled fuselage, sweptback wings, low-set tail, jutting engine inlets

ABOVE
Emblazoned with 'Thuds Forever' on a wing tank, and with various other unofficial markings, Peach 91 – an F-105F of the Georgia Air National Guard – flies the last official Thud mission

FAR LEFT
Shark-mouthed Thuds, aligned on the ramp at Dobbins AFB, Georgia, are being readied by ground crews as the flight crews arrive. The 116th TFW is a crack unit of the Air National Guard

LEFT
On the characteristic paving of the Korat ramp stands 'Damn Okie', an F-105F (62-4427) of the 561st TFS, 23rd TFW. A Standard ARM is carried under the left wing and two Shrikes on the outboard pylons

ABOVE
Bathed in the golden glow of the late-afternoon sun two F-105Ds from the 36th TFW orbit above the cloud cover near their Bitburg, Germany, base

ABOVE RIGHT
How could an aircraft this pretty ever have been called the Thud?

RIGHT
This line-up of Air Force Reserve Thuds of the 466th TFS (Diamondbacks) at Hill AFB is headed by 'My Karma', the commander's aircraft, with its unusual "charcoal lizard" camouflage scheme

RIGHT
Three Thuds in three different camouflage schemes from the 466th TFS, Hill AFB. All are in low-visibility markings, representative of European, Desert and Southeast Asia

BELOW RIGHT
A mixed batch of F-105Ds from the 333rd TFS and an F from the 357th TFS, both of the 355th TFW, take on fuel from a KC-135A tanker during a northbound mission

BELOW LEFT
With a Standard ARM missile under the right wing, an F-105G Wild Weasel (63-8266) from the 17th WWS, 388th TFW out of Korat, turns toward the target area

BELOW
An F-105G Wild Weasel of the Georgia Air National Guard roars off, afterburner in full cry

The front cockpit of the Thud, crammed with instruments,
knobs and switches in every square inch

deep into the north, and had been in a fight with some MiGs. In doing so they had burned more fuel than they had expected to, so they called for any tanker available to meet them half-way. One tanker crew heard and headed towards the four at maximum speed. When they met, two of the pilots were ready to eject; their fuel state was at a couple of hundred pounds, enough to take the Thud around the block once, maybe.

The tanker hooked the fourth plane in the flight first; he had only 100 pounds showing on the gauge, and the boomer hit him while both planes were still turning for position. He took on just enough fuel to keep going, then broke contact and the leader – whose gauges by then were reading empty – hooked up next. The sharp boomer hit all four fighters in turn, giving each just enough fuel to sustain it for a few minutes until the others had been supplied; thus all four of them were saved. It's worth recording that the tanker was a Boeing KC-135A from the 301st Air Refuelling Squadron, with SAC crew T-89, commanded by Captain Howard G. Stalnecker.

F-105s out of Takhli could not reach the combat areas at all without additional fuel, but with it, they were limited only by their target location. The squadrons at Korat, farther east, could go on unrefuelled low-risk missions over Laos, but had only enough fuel for a few minutes in the combat area.

So the pilot's took on their fuel – typically, an 8,000-pound load – thanked the boomer, said good-day, and continued north-north-east to the border of North Vietnam. They had been cruising at about 480 knots to that point, but once over the border, they would notch the throttle up until the air-speed tape read 540 knots; then they would start to become very aware. Turning on to an east-north-east heading, they soon saw the line of hills north-west of Hanoi, pointing straight at the city. That was Thud Ridge and at its end lay Phuc Yen, one of Hanoi's airports, and the home of an aggressive MiG outfit.

The MiGs would wait in orbits north-west and south-west of Hanoi; the Thuds had to come in and go out in one or both of those directions. When they were heading downtown, the MiG would try to jump them to make them jettison their bombs and try to fight; it took a great deal of discipline not to dump everything and head for the deck in full afterburner, with the MiG losing ground every second.

There is the target; now you exert some back pressure and the Thud begins to climb, heading for the sky in the first stage of your bombing run. You establish the run-in altitude, push over and dive at the target, pickle the bomb at about 7,000 feet, start the pull-out and you're straight and level and going like hell at about 4,500 feet. The

'They never gave up trying to rebuild Dien Bien Phu,'
Broughton wrote. 'These are secondary fuel explosions (bright
spots) following a direct hit.' The strike camera recorded the
bomb impact, one of the hundreds, perhaps thousands, to have
hit the site

This is what interdiction was about: A winding road across the Plain des Jarres, with truck traffic widely separated. Some cover for vehicles and drivers; hardly a 100-yard straight stretch to simplify the attack

tapes tell you that you're over the Mach, bowling along faster than the speed of sound. You are executing the classic defensive maneuver called GTHO (Get the Hell Out), while keeping a lookout for MiGs, SAM, terrain, anything. Then you are past the defenses, safe again, and you begin to decelerate to form up on the lead.

Next it's back over Laos, cruise towards Thailand, hit the tankers again just over the border and settle down for the approach and the landing and the O-Club and the pool.

At least part of the thrill of that ride – typically, a three-hour excursion – was removed when the electronic countermeasures (ECM) pods became available in quantity early in 1967. They worked so well that the flights penetrated at 15,000 feet, safe from SAMs and the heavier AAA and probably safe from MiGs. Every North-Vietnamese early-warning, GCI and guidance radar was displaying a screen full of noise.

Punching the Dragon's Jaw

Thanh Hoa village, about 75 miles south of Hanoi, was the site of the Ham Rong (the words means dragon's jaw and relate to an elaborate Vietnamese legend) railroad and highway bridge, spanning the Song Ma river. It had twin steel through-truss spans set on nine concrete piers and the center pier was 16 feet in diameter. Its ends were anchored in concrete abutments between 30 and 40 feet thick. It was defended by nearby 37mm AAA positions.

Rolling Thunder Mission 9-Alpha was flown against the Ham Rong bridge on 3 April 1965. The strike force was sent north just after noon and its 78 aircraft included 31 F-105s from the 67th TFS – whose commander, Lt-Col Robinson Risner, also commanded the strike force – and the 355th TFW. Another 15 F-105s were along for defense-suppression. Thirty of the Thuds carried the standard load of 750 lb general purpose (GP) bombs; the remaining 16 carried Bullpup missiles. Those 16, plus 15 bombers, were to attack the bridge; the remainder, the flak. The first aircraft made their initial run in against the bridge at about 14.00hrs, were hammered by the flak and didn't get the bridge. The Bullpup missile was a spectacular failure; its warhead was too light to damage the structure. The subsequent Navy strike a few hours later had no more luck with the target, either. However, the Navy mission was bounced by three MiG-17 fighters, bearing the red-outlined yellow star of the North Vietnamese Air Force. It was a foretaste of what was to come.

The restrike was scheduled for the next day. The force mix included 35 F-105s, drawn from the 18th and 355th TFWs, loaded with 750 lb GP bombs. Eight F-100s flew flak-suppression and two more went ahead for weather reconnaissance. Bullpup missiles had not been loaded,

This Thud, a D-10RE, serial 60-0498, shows one of the standard weapons configurations for the war: Six 750 lb M117 general-purpose bombs

ABOVE
Northbound, this F-105D-10RE carries a Bullpup B under the
starboard wing. The aircraft is from the 33rd TFS, 355th TFW,
based at Takhli

LEFT
The crew chief snaps a salute to the boss, Col. Jack Broughton,
vice commander of the 355th TFW at Takhli, as Broughton
eases his Thud off the ramp. The F-105D-31RE is a late
production model, serial 62-4338, the 537th D model built, and
is loaded with 750 pounders and 450-gallon wing tanks

the previous mission having proved their relative
uselessness against that kind of target.

The Thuds left their bases at Korat and Takhli,
rendezvoused with their tankers and refuelled over the
Mekong river and headed across Laos to the IP (Initial
Point) some three minutes south of the Ham Rong
bridge. They turned north there and soon had the bridge
in sight. The flights had been spaced with great care so
that each wave could make its attack and clear the target
area for the next aircraft. One by one, the Thuds rolled in
towards the north-west, planning to cross the bridge at
about a 20-degree angle and drop.

Lt-Col Risner, again commanding the strike force, flew
the lead F-105D. He was first into the attack, pushed into
a dive, sighted on the bridge and released the clutch of
bombs. He pulled out of his dive and headed for a perch
above the battle, rather than going into full afterburner
and staying low to clear the area. He had been ordered to
hang around after his run-in, to observe and direct the
strikes. As he watched, the next pilot – Capt Carlyle S.

ABOVE
The six Mk-82 500-lb Snakeye high-drag bombs are loaded,
and the Thud has been fueled ready for a Northbound mission

LEFT
Escape kit, pistol, tourniquets and bandages, dye marker,
mirror, ammo, and a long list of other personal gear is pocketed
in every reachable place on the flying suit and the vest.

Harris – pushed into his dive, released his Thud's eight
bombs at about 4,000 feet and pulled into a gut-straining
recovery at about 1,000 feet.

Just off the target, Harris' Thud was hit in the aft
fuselage and seemed to stop and pirouette in the air. Its
left wing tank was torn off and the warning lights began
to glow yellow on the annunciator panel. Harris was able
to eject, but he was captured and then spent seven years in
prisoner-of-war camps.

Zinc flight was scheduled to strike last. The four
F-105Ds from the 67th TFS at Korat had arrived ahead
of their scheduled attack time, and were waiting at the IP
for clearance to go in and strike when they were bounced
by four MiG-17s diving out of the low clouds. The little
silver fighters made a pass through the Thud formation,
their cannon chattering. Zinc Lead and Zinc Two were
hit on the first pass and both pilots were lost, so the score
was three to nothing against the USAF – and the bridge
still stood.

The Thuds had suffered their first losses to enemy
aircraft in the USAF's first air battle of that war, but the
strike against the Ham Rong bridge was also noteworthy
for other reasons. It marked the introduction of hit-and-
run air combat tactics by the North Vietnamese; it was
influential in defining the composition of later strike
packages; and it was instrumental in causing a rethinking
of the weapons loads.

Bomb-damage assessment pictures showed that about
300 bombs had hit the bridge at various points, but none
had done serious harm, let alone dropped a span. It was
very obvious that 750-lb bombs were of as little value as
the Bullpups against the heavily built bridge. Bigger
bombs, and more, if possible, were seen as a solution, but
there was a problem in increasing the ordnance load on
the Thuds. They could carry an enormous weight, but
didn't. The drag of the external bomb array degraded
their performance to such an extent that hot-day take-offs
became critical ('like a cross-country trip on the ground,'
said one pilot). Further, with a sizeable bomb load, the

Thud couldn't struggle up to usual refuelling altitudes. The tankers had to go down to 15,000 feet to enable them to refuel.

Consequently, the Thuds were loaded with only a relative handful of 750-lb bombs, usually seven. It looked ridiculous to be carrying such a load, but it was the best operational compromise. And there was another factor bearing on the number of bombs loaded: the moment anybody in the strike formation spotted MiGs, the alarm went up and all ordnance was jettisoned immediately. It was tough enough to manoeuvre and evade with an empty Thud, let alone one that was loaded with the weight and drag penalties of bombs. So, since the final goal of a mission was bombs on target, not MiG wreckage on the ground, it was considered preferable to take the chance of jettisoning seven 750-pounders in preference to a much-higher bomb load. A periodic bomb shortage, always denied by the Pentagon but confirmed on the scene, contributed to that logic.

There was another, and almost immediate, reaction to the first loss of F-105s over the north. Lockheed EC-121D Constellation (College Eye) aircraft were deployed to south-east Asia to support the strike forces with early detection and warning of enemy MiG activity. Surface radars weren't able to do that job, lacking both range and the ability to see into North Vietnam, but the long-range airborne early-warning radars of the College Eye could and their plots prevented subsequent surprise attacks.

In addition to being heavy and therefore considerably more leaden-footed than the nimble MiG-17s, the F-105

was not blessed with much visibility aft from the cockpit. So it may come as a surprise to find that their record as MiG-killers was unexpectedly good. Here's how their first one was logged.

On 29 June 1966, the 388th TFW had dispatched, among others, four F-105Ds to fly an Iron Hand mission with a strike force. Iron Hand aircraft had the unenviable task of knocking out, or otherwise suppressing, the surface-to-air missiles operated by the Communist forces. They were working over some targets north-north-west of Hanoi when four MiG-17s attacked from the seven o'clock position just as the flight lead and his wingman, Maj Fred L. Tracy, were turning left off the target. Lead and Tracy slammed throttles into full afterburner, jettisoned their ordnance and broke hard left into diving turns. The first MiG pilot triggered a burst as he flashed by the third and fourth Thuds, also diving hard in full afterburner and, with his wingman, chased Tracy and his leader.

ABOVE
Back from combat, the centerline rack is empty, and access doors are opened for the myriad of tasks needed to turn the aircraft round overnight. Two technicians are removing the ammunition drum ready to be reloaded

LEFT
Technicians work on the 20-mm Vulcan cannon while this Thud is being refuelled during a turnaround

The lead MiG got a clean shot at Tracy, damaged his instruments, his gunsight and his oxygen equipment and knocked his hand off the throttle. That took the big J75 out of afterburner, so the Thud decelerated, and the MiG overshot. Tracy positioned himself easily at the MiG's six o'clock and fired about 200 rounds at the yellow-starred fighter. The damaged MiG rolled inverted and split-essed into cloud cover at about 2,000 feet. The likelihood of his recovery was nil, so Tracy was credited with the first MiG-17 kill by a Thud pilot.

On 18 August, Maj Kenneth T. Blank, 34th TFS, had a very similar experience. He was also on Iron Hand when his flight sighted two MiGs, one breaking into an attack on the lead Thud. Blank, flying wing to the lead, flung the Thud into the MiG's six o'clock and thumbed the trigger; a short burst from the M61 hammered the MiG from about 400 feet and it flamed, dived and slammed into the ground.

First Lt Karl W. Richter, 23 years old and the youngest USAF pilot to shoot down a MiG-17, became a legend after completing more than 200 combat missions up north and succumbing during an otherwise successful rescue. He 'killed' his first MiG – and the third for the Thuds – on 21 September. He was flying lead of the second element of a four-plane Iron Hand mission from the 338th out of Korat, when the lead element was attacked by a pair of MiG-17s. Richter and his wingman turned into the MiGs and Richter opened fire at about 2,000 feet, hitting the first aircraft.

The Communist pilot rolled out of his left turn into a hard right turn, and his wingman broke to the left. The Thuds stayed with their original target, the lead MiG,

117

RIGHT
It bent the leading-edge spar a little and blew a large hole in the upper and lower skins, but the enemy warhead didn't stop this Thud

FAR RIGHT
The suggestion is that this Thud was hit by a Russian-built Atoll missile. Not Atoll; Sidewinder. The aircraft was hit by a friendly missile, but happily got home again. It proves that the Thud was strongly built. The Thud is a D-10RE, serial 60-5376

BELOW
Some of these holes can be patched simply; others are going to take more work

and Richter fired again. The 20mm shells hit the right wing, which ripped off straightaway; as Richter flew past the decelerating MiG, the pilot ejected.

On the same day, four F-105Ds from the 335th out of Takhli were attacking the Dap Cau bridge when they spotted a MiG at their 12 o'clock low position. The lead Thud and his wingman dived to the attack and the leader fired, damaging the MiG, but its pilot was able to slam into afterburner, pull up and roll into the six o'clock on the Thud leader. The second Thud in the element was piloted by First Lt Fred A. Wilson Jr, who charged off to the rescue, firing continuously. His gunnery shot off part of the MiG's rear fuselage and, after banking into a tight left turn, Wilson saw an explosion on the ground where the MiG could have hit.

RIGHT
Souvenir of Hanoi, this flak hole in Broughton's Thud is right through the leading edge of the vertical fin, missing the spar and fortunately leaving him with directional control of his Thud. 'It was ready to go the next day, with a complete new fin,' said Broughton

BELOW
After release this Thud's drop-tank reared up and struck the leading edge. The aircraft returned, safely, to base where it was repaired and returned to combat

Maj Roy S. Dickey scored the last of the 1966 MiG victories for the Thud on 4 December. He was flying one of four F-105Ds on a strike against rail yards a few miles north of Hanoi when four MiGs got between them and the target. Dickey made his bomb run and then saw one of the MiGs firing at a Thud just below him and about half a mile ahead.

He closed the gap to 700 feet or so and opened fire. Flame shot out of the wing roots and then the fuselage aft of the cockpit blazed brightly. The MiG rolled into a right-hand spin, burning all the way down to 3,500 feet, where Dickey last saw him before he was interrupted by another MiG, firing from his six o'clock. The Thud responded to Dickey's fervent manoeuvring, and headed for the deck in a steep dive. He leveled out at 50 feet, going like the hammers of Hell, and never saw the MiG again.

The final score for 1966 was five MiGs for the F-105 pilots. 1967 was even better: the F-105 aircrews scored $22\frac{1}{2}$ victories in air-to-air combat over the agile MiG-17. On two different dates, 19 April and 13 May, the Thuds accounted for four MiG-17s in one day. It was a formidable record, and was achieved primarily by gunfire. Of the $27\frac{1}{2}$ victories, 25 were due to gunfire from the 20mm M61, the very cannon that was going to be removed from the aircraft because '...its effectiveness had

not been established.' Two MiG-17s were shot down with AIM-9 Sidewinders launched by F-105D pilots and one was brought low by a combination of an AIM-9 and gunfire.

It was small consolation knowing that the enemy had lost almost 28 MiG-17s when the other side of the coin was examined. During 1966, the year in which the Thuds shot down just five MiG-17s, the USAF lost 85 F-105s, 31 during the first six months, and 54 during the latter six. Late in 1967, the Air Force announced that it had lost between 325 and 330 F-105s over North Vietnam. It was a low loss rate, taken on a percentage basis – only 1·6 aircraft per 1,000 sorties – but the sorties were running at a high level, and 10,000 of them meant 16 Thuds gone forever, and 100,000 of them meant 160. By August 1968, Thud losses had climbed so high that the authorized squadron strengths in the 355th and 388th TFWs, normally set at 24 aircraft, had been reduced by one-quarter to 18.

In less than 10 years, the total strength of 833 production F-105 aircraft of all types had been cut by losses in battle and other causes to 427. There was no longer a production line for the them, although Republic tried valiantly for reopen it and although Thud pilots devoutly wished for more in the pipeline. The light at the end of the tunnel was the setting sun for the Thud.

6
Lightning Rods

The mission of the Wild Weasel crews was simply stated: protect the strike force by suppressing enemy air defense systems. Wild Weasel crews flew as a team, in a two-seat fighter-bomber modified with special electronic equipment. The pilot and his 'Bear' – the nickname given to all the Weasel backseaters – preceded the strike force into the areas most heavily defended by missiles and flak. They tempted those defenses, waiting for them to fire. Their first warning might be a sudden rattling – it has been likened, appropriately, to the sound a rattlesnake makes just before it strikes – of the radar homing and warning equipment, heard in their headsets, and the simultaneous appearance of a blip on the scope of the warning receiver.

Their reactions had to be swift. In one practised sequence, the crew swung the plane into a tight evasive manoeuvre, scanned the horizon for the first tell-tale smoke of a missile launch, looking into the sky for enemy fighters, warned any other friendly aircraft of the threat, and preparing to do battle with the enemy. There might be MiGs overhead, waiting; there might be decoy signals, or multiple batteries, with one holding fire while the other attracted the Weasels' attention. After clearing a route to the target for the strike force, they orbited in a low-threat area, waiting around to clear the skies again for the safe exit of the bombers. Whatever happened, it was the most dangerous game of all, and every sortie was a flight into the jaws.

How dangerous? During all of the long war in southeast Asia, only a dozen USAF personnel performed such selfless acts as to deserve the Medal of Honor, America's highest award for valor. Two of those recipients were F-105 pilots and both were Wild Weasels.

Republic F-105F and F-105G models, specially modified for the mission, carried most of the Wild Weasel

After the active units shed the F-105Gs in favour of F-4G Weasels, the Georgia ANG was assigned the mission. Shown is 63-8265 with Shrikes mounted on outboard pylons

crews on their dangerous sorties. Here's how the mission and the aircraft evolved.

Background to the Wild Weasel mission

The basic Wild Weasel mission of suppressing the enemy's defenses can be traced back to World War II and, specifically, to the daring flights by pilots of four USAAF fighter groups. The Allies had scheduled an airborne assault against German positions in the Netherlands in an operation designated Market Garden. This combined British and American airborne infantry and paratroops who were to reach their positions by glider landings and by parachute drops; both were very vulnerable to well directed anti-aircraft fire of which the Germans had a larger variety and concentration.

Four fighter groups – the 56th, 78th, 353rd and 356th – dispatched their pilots in Republic P-47 Thunderbolts to positions on the inbound route of the aerial armada that would be bringing in the infantry. The P-47 pilots were to loiter in the area, in weather that reduced their changes of spotting the enemy gun positions and wait until they were fired upon. The idea was that they could then, locate the offending battery and attack it. It was extremely dangerous and the losses were frightful. The 56th Fighter Group sent out 39 pilots on one of those suicidal missions, and only 23 returned. It was the worse loss of the war for the Group, but their sacrifices contributed to a safer trip in for the infantry.

In the Vietnam war, the concept was re-invented after the first losses of USAF fighters. Zinc Lead and Zinc Two were the first to fall, hit by MiG-17s and that MiG attack was the first indication of a co-ordinated air interception effort against the north-bound raiders.

The next day, 5 April 1965, a strategic reconnaissance flight discovered the first known enemy surface-to-air missile (SAM) launch site, under construction 15 miles south-east of Hanoi. By mid July, five more had been visually identified and during a mission north, one of the EB-66C electronic intelligence (ELINT) gatherers had

intercepted guidance signals clearly coming from missile radars; the suspected locus was a new one, a missile site west of Hanoi.

On 24 July, a flight of McDonnell F-4Cs from Ubon, MIGCAP to a strike force, heard a missile warning flashed by an EB-66 which had intercepted guidance signals; the site west of Hanoi was on the air. Within seconds, a SAM streaked upwards and blew a Phantom out of the sky. Two more missiles detonated behind the flight and the remaining three aircraft were peppered with shrapnel, but they were able to get back to base safely.

The loss of that F-4C, 55 miles north-west of Hanoi, near the village of Lang Chi, was the first warning of heavier losses to come. The specific SAM was a Russian-developed SA-2, code-named Guideline by NATO, a first-generation surface-to-air missile. It used a radio command guidance system that required continuous tracking of both the target and the missile by ground radar (designated Fan Song by NATO), carried a 100kg high-explosive warhead and had a slant range of between 25 and 30 miles. Its liquid-fuelled sustainer rocket left a smoke trail by day, and a fiery trail by night, something which rendered it at a disadvantage, because US pilots could spot it at great distances.

The Air Force response was immediate. An Air Staff Task Force, led by Brig-Gen K.C. Dempster, Deputy for Operational Requirements and Development Plans in USAF Headquarters, was appointed to study methods of countering the air defense system in North Vietnam. The Task Force seminar, held in August, led to a recommendation for the development of a specialized aircraft that could detect, locate and destroy enemy air defense system radars. The code name for this new mission concept: Wild Weasel.

To understand the part that the modified F-105F and the further modified F-105G played in the unique combat experience as Wild Weasels, it's helpful to look at

some of the tactics and equipment developed to counter the superlative air defence system deployed in the field by the North Vietnamese army units.

RHAW (pronounced 'raw' and standing for radar homing and warning) equipment existed; Itek AN/APR-25 and similar units were in production and available for installation. They could detect an enemy radar that was 'painting' an aircraft, and indicate its bearing. They were being installed as routine modifications in a number of tactical aircraft, but a small batch of fighter-bombers was being modified for a special mission.

On 21 November, the first four of seven North American two-seat F-100F Wild Weasel conversions arrived at Korat, Royal Thai Air Force Base (RTAFB) on TDY. They had been attached to the 33th TFW at Eglin AFB and, after their deployment, were assigned to operate as part of the 388th TFW at Korat. Teamed with F-105Ds carrying iron bombs, the Weasels began flying Iron Hand attack missions against missile sites on 3 December, but the Thuds and Super Sabres were not a well matched team. The F-100s could not carry enough bomb-load to mount an effective attack alone; their AGM-45A Shrike missiles were not very reliable and the F-105 was a much-faster aircraft.

Between late July and the bombing halt on 24 December 1965, 180 SAMs were fired, according to US pilot reports. They destroyed 11 aircraft. Each kill thus required an average of more than 16 missiles, but it was a start for the enemy. Tacticians pointed out that the kill probability of each missile was six percent, and that figure was high enough to cause much concern at this early stage of SAM operations.

When US air strikes resumed on 1 February, they were opposed by a fully integrated air defense system. It was primarily a numerically increased air defense threat which led to the development of advanced Wild Weasel systems. The poor quality of the Russian-built missiles and the inadequately trained crews hampered the North Vietnamese batteries somewhat, but the combination of electronic countermeasures (ECM) and evasive tactics used by USAF crews was the best parry to the missiles' thrust. Best, that is, in the sense that they reduced the probability of SAM kills. However, they were tactically less than satisfactory.

Through bitter and daring experience, USAF pilots had learned that the SAMs could be outmanoeuvred, if seen in time. They learned to judge just when to break towards the missile in a hard, diving turn, followed by a

LEFT
The earliest Thud Weasels were F models like this one, the 116th F-105F-1RE, serial 63-8339. She's named 'Road Runner', after the cartoon bird. In service with the 357th TFS, 355th TFW, Takhli, and armed with AGM-45A Shrike missiles

BELOW
Recognition feature of the F-105G Wild Weasel, a conversion of the F models, was the AN/ALQ-105 blister on each side of the fuselage just above the bomb-bay doors

4g abrupt rolling pull-up. The rugged Thud excelled at this kind of low-level, gut-wrenching manoeuver. The missile was unable to follow the sequence and missed to detonate well away from them. There was a drawback though: the pilots lived, but the targets did too. At the first transmission of 'SAM! SAM! Take her down!', anyone who suspected he was in line for a missile shot jettisoned his ordnance and headed for the ground. Therefore, to achieve a higher percentage of completed strikes, Air Force pilots developed new tactics to avoid, rather than evade, the SAMs.

They began their attack runs with a low-level approach, hugging the terrain and using it to mask the flight from detection by enemy radars. After passing some known initial point (IP), the pilots timed their runs and, at a predetermined time, pulled up into a steep climb, followed by a half-roll so that the target could be spotted visually. Then the F-105 was pulled down and half-rolled again and the target attacked in a dive. That tactical procedure had two inbuilt snags: the low-altitude segment was within the reach of small-arms fire and AAA and the pop-up put the planes right within the SAM

envelope. Clearly, there was a need for a new combination of tactics and technology to decrease the continuing SAM threat.

The solution led to the development of the F-105F two-seater into an advanced Wild Weasel, armed with missiles that would ride the enemy radar back to its source. The best missile then available was the AGM-45A Shrike, which had been the first of the anti-radiation weapons in the US arsenal, having been developed by the Navy in 1961 solely for the purpose of defeating Russian surface-to-air radars.

The first 13 F-105Fs converted to Wild Weasel configuration had arrived at Korat by the summer of 1966, followed by 10 more F-105F models sent to Takhli RTAFB during the three months following. Soon after their arrival, however, the F-100F Wild Weasels were withdrawn from service; only two of the original seven had survived their missions.

The new F-105Fs flew two basic missions as Wild Weasels. The first was as a member of a hunter-killer team, accompanied by other fighter-bombers which were either F-105Ds or F-4s. The second was as a member of a strike force support package, to escort and protect the bombers.

In the endless cycle of offensive and defensive moves which are modern war, the North Vietnamese quickly derived a counter to the Wild Weasel/ Shrike combination. They coordinated missile radars with long-range ground-controlled intercept or early-warning

radars. The missile radars stayed off the air, doing no tracking, but keeping warm by working against a dummy load. When warned by the more-powerful radars that a strike force was coming in, the SAM sites would go on the air just long enough to verify the aiming and launch, switching off again immediately. In that brief time, it was often impossible for the Weasels to detect, locate and hit or mark them.

The Air Force response was the introduction of electronic countermeasures, specifically jamming pods that could be carried on wing pylons of selected aircraft in the attacking force. Their emissions jammed the enemy

ABOVE
WA 432 is a Wild Weasel F-105G, modified and equipped with the latest anti-missile systems

LEFT
Seen from the front, the AN/ALQ-105 blister

radars, confusing them as to the range and bearing of the strike force. With their new, invisible shields, the F-105 bombers could fly straight and level at altitudes of 12,000 to 15,000 feet, jamming as they went, and roll in on the target for dive-bombing in the conventional fashion.

At the beginning of 1967, even though there were by then at least 170 known SAM sites up north, the ECM pods were earning their keep. Carrying them meant that one pylon was useless for weapons, but this mattered little, because a much higher percentage of weapons loaded could be delivered, instead of jettisoned. By flying carefully planned formations, with vertical and lateral

separations determined and rigidly held, a strike force could deny range, and bearing and altitude information to the enemy ground radars, effectively blinding the eyes of a powerful air defense system.

In early April 1968, the USAF had its target territory limited to the southern portion of North Vietnam. That region had few SAM sites and very few targets. So, even though the F-105s were now loaded with the new and better Standard ARM anti-radar missile, introduced in March 1968, there were few chances to fire.

Casualty rates continued to be high, a sad but not surprising fact. On 24 September 1970, the surviving

Weasels at the de-activating Takhli air base flew to Korat and reformed as Detachment 1 of the 12th TFS. In November they were organized and re-designated as the 6010th Wild Weasel Squadron (WWS), which, a year later, was again re-designated as the 17th WWS. It continued to operate alone in the theater until April 1972, when it was joined by the deployed 561st TFS, from the F-105 training base at McConnell AFB, Kansas.

It should be recorded that some F-4C and F-4D aircraft were converted to Wild Weasel configuration. The former were sent to Pacific Air Forces (PACAF) in October, 1969, and stationed at Osan AB, Korea; the latter pioneered the AN/APR-38 system, later to be the central feature of the F-4G Wild Weasel, in late 1972, too late to see action in south-east Asia.

May of 1972 saw the beginning of the Linebacker I air offensive. By then, attrition had reduced the number of F-105Ds available and the strike forces were being built around the F-4, but the Wild Weasel force had been strengthened by the arrival of more-capable F-105G aircraft, modified from F models, which had the increased strike powers of the Standard ARM missile.

A typical strike package put up 32 F-4s loaded with a mix of conventional and laser-guided bombs, and

ABOVE
In July, 1978, the 'Hanoi Hustler', still complete with three red stars, was photographed at George AFB, while on the strength of the 562nd TFS, 35th TFW. 'Hanoi Hustler' is carrying a rocket launcher pod on the starboard outboard pylon. The adjacent Weasel, 63-8328, is carrying an instrumentation pod on the port pylon for missions on the ACMI (Air Combat Manoeuvring Instrumentation) range at Nellis AFB

ABOVE RIGHT
Wild Weasel F-105G, 63-8266, from the 18th TFW, at Kadena AB, Japan, carries AGM-45 Shrikes outboard and AGM-78 Standard ARMs inboard

LEFT
A Weasel from the 561st TFS, formating on a tanker over south east Asia, carries three red stars signifying kills. Named the 'Hanoi Hustler', 63-8320 (see above), this aircraft served with both the 17th TFS and the 561st.

escorted by between 20 and 40 supporting aircraft. The available F-105s were given the support task, with four Wild Weasels out ahead of the strike force to search for the SAM sites. Hunter-killer teams, pairing the Weasel Thuds with Phantoms, were assigned to suppress SAMs and the anti-aircraft artillery. The Weasels carried no bombs. Their outboard pylons held two Shrikes and on inboard pylon mounted a Standard ARM. Those three missiles, and the 20mm cannon, were the magic amulet for the Thuds.

Thud crews detected and located the SAMs and their controlling radars and then fired one or more of the missiles to mark the target and put the radar off the air. The F-4 fighter-bombers, loaded with cluster and iron bombs, then swung in to wipe out the site. The Phantoms, being the better air-to-air bird, also carried Sidewinder air-to-air missiles to protect the Wild Weasels from interceptors.

By the end of July 1972, the inventory of F-105G aircraft had been reduced to fewer than a dozen in the 561st TFS (Wild Weasels) and about 20 in the 17th WWS. Linebacker II, the heavy bomber offensive mounted in December 1972, was the last hurrah for the Weasels. In those raids, eight F-105F and F-105G Wild Weasels worked through the night as ECM support for the B-52 strikes, flying ahead of, and with, the bomber cells, to suppress the SAMs. They were assisted by some F-4C Wild Weasels from the squadron then at Osan AB. Strategic Air Command had specifically asked for that kind of help after its initial experience with outdated bombing tactics. The Weasel Thuds were limited by their performance to altitudes below 18,000 feet and sometimes found themselves in the middle of bomb drops.

At the end of the war, the two Weasel squadrons were returned to the United States with the three dozen F-105Gs that had survived the battles. The 561st TFS was assigned to the 35th TFW, George AFB, California, in the autumn of 1973. The 17th WWS, the last operator of the Thud in the south-east Asian war theater, was deployed to George AFB a year later. The last F-105G of the 17th departed from Korat on 29 October, 1974,

concluding 10 years of F-105 service in south-east Asia, eight of them in combat. The squadron was then disbanded and its assets incorporated into the newly formed 562nd TFS of the 35th TFW. Each F-105 squadron of the 35th had an authorized strength of 18 aircraft.

The Weasel Thuds continued to serve with TAC's 35th TFW in the 561st and 562nd TFS and with the 563rd Tactical Fighter Training Squadron. The last-named of these was equipped with a mix of F-105G and F-4C Wild Weasel aircraft. The last F-105Gs on the USAF active force roster began to be phased out on 28 April, 1978, when TAC accepted the first production F-4G, successor to the long line of Wild Weasels.

Development of the F-105F Wild Weasel

In late 1965, tactical aircraft in south-east Asia were field-modified with installations of RHAW systems, specifically, the AN/APR-25 and -26 receivers. The purpose was to increase pilots' capabilities to avoid, or to attack, the radar-directed SAMs and AAA. Included among the types modified were both the single-seat F-105Ds and the two-seater F-105Fs.

ABOVE
This 18th TFW, F-105G Wild Weasel, 63-8333, shows the installation of Standard ARM and Shrike missiles on its starboard pylons. The Standard ARM seeker head is protected by a cylindrical cover

ABOVE LEFT
Returning from the target a mixed gaggle of Weasels from the 561st and 17th TFS (tail codes WW and JB respectively) are accompanied by two McDonnell F-4s from the 34th TFS. All are from the 388th TFW, Korat RTAFB

The 1965 Wild Weasel I program, which modified and put into service the first batch of F-100F (WW) aircraft, also included the same modifications for 86 of the F-105Fs that had previously been equipped with the RHAW gear. In January 1966, the F-105F Wild Weasel modifications began, and the new equipment included:

AN/APR-25 vector crystal video receiver, made by Itek and used to detect S-band emissions from the SA-2, early-warning and GCI radars, C-band radiations from the improved SA-2 radars, and X-band characteristics of the airborne intercept radars (the information warned the pilot when he was being tracked by enemy radars, and displayed a coarse relative bearing to the threat).
AN/APR-26 (WR-300) crystal video L-band warning receiver, made by Itek and used to sense a power-level change in the L-band command guidance radar of the SAM; IR-133 panoramic receiver to detect S-band emissions at long range;
KA-60 panoramic camera;
dual-track combat-event tape recorder.

Adding a new offensive or defensive weapon system to an aircraft is not a simple task. It involves tests of

131

compatibility with existing equipment, cross-checks for possible radio or other signal interference, test firings and a program of evaluation and acceptance tests. The F-105F was initially only modified to handle the AGM-45A Shrike missile; the Standard ARM anti-radiation weapons were still in the future.

Accordingly, 14 of the 86 F-105F(WW) aircraft were further modified to be able to fire the Standard ARM Mod 0, in a program that was completed in February 1968. The modification included the installation of a Bendix AN/APS-107 unit, which located, identified and acquired the radiating target and presented that data to the Standard ARM guidance system. Additionally, an Itek AN/APR-35 unit provided the acquisition capability for the missile. In the following month, the last of the Wild Weasel III modifications was completed on the F-105F(WW) aircraft, updating those planes with current models of the RHAW receivers, units that were in a constant state of flux as enemy radar operations and frequencies changed. The F-105Fs also carried active ECM equipment, including the AN/ALQ-59 jammer developed from the QRC-128 unit, and the AN/ALQ-71

noise jammer, a spin-off from the QRC-160-1 equipment.

Finally, 16 F-105F(WW) were the subjects for one more set of modifications. The program began in November 1968 and was completed the following June. When it was completed, those 16 could fire the newest Standard ARM Mod 1 and their airframes housed other equipment that was also destined for an additional 60 F-105F(WW) aircraft, to be redesignated F-105G.

One of the reasons for these small-batch modifications was that there weren't that many two-seat Thuds around to adapt. Republic had built only 143 of them and attrition and combat losses had taken their toll. In fact, F-105F airframes were so rare that the operational squadrons were authorized UE (Unit Establishment) strengths of only 18 aircraft, instead of the usual 24.

Development of the F-105G

The last upgrading and modification of the F model was followed by a major program to produce a reasonably large number of standardized Wild Weasel aircraft, with common and standardized equipment. The Air Force issued Technical Order 1F-105-1133, dated 23 February 1970: *Modification and Redesignation of F-105F Aircraft to F-105G Configuration.* It called for two prototypes and 51 production conversions to the F-105G, and identified them by serial numbers. The equipment to be installed was one generation later than the units on the Fs and was accordingly more capable. It could look at the signal characteristics of the enemy radar and tell his intentions, as well as giving the distance to the site instead of just the

bearing. The new system did, however, make greater demands on the Bear. The changes included the installation of:

improved Wild Weasel III capability, including the installation of the Itek AN/APR-35, -36 and -37 RHAW systems, the latter two improvements on the APR-26 and -27, with their displays and controls orientated towards the use of the Standard ARM missile;
AN/ALR-31 RHAW receiver (Project SEE SAM), developed by Loral Electronics under QRC-317;
an Itek ER-142, or equivalent, high-sensitivity wide-band tuned RF crystal video receiver, which gave automatic direction-finding and homing on the threat;
AGM-78B (Mod 1) Standard ARM capability;
14-channel combat-event tape recorder;
AN/ALQ-105 ECM blisters;
QRC-373 ECM capability.

A Wild Weasel aircraft might require up to 13 antennae: four circularly polarized spirals for homing guidance, two conical omni-direction types for search, four directional forward-mounted units for additional homing data, two others for direction-finding and a launch-warning blade type.

There has been some question about the actual number of F-105G conversions. The intention of the Air Force was as stated in the original issue of TO-1133: Two prototypes and 51 production conversions. The C change of the TO, dated 15 May 1970, deleted two aircraft from the list of production conversions, leaving 49. A further

change, TO-1133D of 1 July 1971, added a dozen to the list. There was, therefore, a final total of 61 serially identified aircraft to be converted from F-105F to F-105G.

The rationale behind housing the ECM equipment in blisters on the fuselage sides arose out of the needs of combat. The ECM pods normally carried on a wing station prohibited that station from being used to carry a weapon and the tactical forces initially opposed the introduction of ECM equipment for that reason. Later, when the need for the pods had reached crisis proportions, they were willing to give up a weapons mount to carry one for self-protection.

The blisters were, basically, halves of a Westinghouse Electric Corporation AN/ALQ-105 ECM pod split on its centreline, and fastened to the fuselage sides below the wings. The idea had been tried earlier, with the QCR-301 ECM units, in a project code-named 'Side Car'.

Republic aerodynamicists were naturally concerned about adding another drag-producing item to the F-105F. Tests showed that the blisters produced an incremental 10 counts of drag (0.0010 Cd) at Mach numbers below 0.85, and 20 counts at Mach numbers above 1.1, into the supersonic range. There was a performance trade-off: 4 drag counts produced a 1 percent decrease in range. The penalty for the side blisters, therefore, was about a $2\frac{1}{2}$ percent range loss subsonically and 5 percent supersonically.

The F-105G models saw service as the war was nearing its close and much was learned in their relatively few combat sorties. Perhaps the most important was that the Bear, the man in the back seat, was reaching his limits of physical and mental performance. Physically, he was under terrific strain: his most likely previous assignment had been as a navigator or electronics warfare officer for SAC and he just was not used to what the tactical pilots called 'all that yankin' and bankin'. In a high-threat environment, he was pushed to handle the number of missiles being launched, track each one long enough to determine its relative threat and to flash warnings. The SAM operators had also been going to school on their enemy and had learned much about deception and tactical use, which further complicated the task of the Bear.

Automation of Wild Weasel process was the obvious answer, and it was one of the reasons that the F-105Gs did not last very long in service after they came home from the war. The automated AN/APR-38, under development for several years and delayed repeatedly, was finally considered ready for installation in a Wild Weasel several years after the war had ended and so the F-105G, with its manually operated systems, was phased out in favor of the development of still another Phantom, the F-4G. Thus, one era of Wild Weaseling was at an end.

In the hangar for periodic inspection and maintenance this F-105G, 63-8313, of the 128th TFS, Georgia ANG, gets close attention from a technician

7
The Storm Abates

In one of the classic feats of the air war, a mixed force of Thuds and Phantoms took on the redoubtable Paul Doumer bridge across the Red River north of Hanoi. The bridge was named after the former Governor-General of French Indochina, who was the driving force behind the establishment of the railway system built by the French at the turn of 20th century. Two of the lines connected Hanoi with the north-west and the north-east sectors of the country, and over their steel rails moved a large proportion of the war materiel that supplied the North Vietnamese armies. Another major portion came to Hanoi by rail from Haiphong, the port about 40 miles to the east. One short line existed almost solely to move steel from the Thai Nguyen plant to Hanoi. All four of those routes crossed the Red River on the Doumer bridge. So did Route Nationale 1, North Vietnam's main highway.

The bridge was a testimonial to French engineering of the time. It was about a mile long, not counting its approach viaducts; it was 38 feet wide, with a single metre-gauge track down its center, and a roadway, 10 feet wide, on each side. There were 18 concrete piers jutting out of the waters of the Red River to support the 19 separate trusswork spans.

The bridge was initially within the boundaries of the restricted attack zones, defined by the Johnson administration, which protected Hanoi and Haiphong. It could not even be chosen as a target, because it was too near to Hanoi, which lay south and west of the span. To the east were Gia Lam airfield and a group of factories. Villages and rice paddies lay in the Red River floodplain to the north.

The bridge was defended by a concentration of multiple SAM batteries, automatic 23mm light flak batteries and units of 37mm, 57mm and 85mm AAA.

AN F-105B-20RE, 57-5837, of the 419th TFW takes-off from Hill AFB, against the dramatic backdrop of the Wasatch mountain range

Radar-directed 85mm batteries guarded each end. The full air strength of the North – a mix of MiG-17 and MiG-21 interceptors and their associated ground-controlled radars – was based only a few minutes away.

It was an obvious choice for a target. To knock down one or more spans would interrupt Hanoi's supply lines both from China and from its port city of Haiphong. It was a difficult target; bridges are long, narrow structures that are hard to hit, even in good weather, with no defenses and no winds. Compounding the problems by adding deadly defense in depth meant that a destruction mission could be expected to be costly and possibly a complete failure.

However, this one was on. Finally, the Rolling Thunder 57 target list included the bridge. Seventh Air Force headquarters sent orders at 10:00am on 11 August 1967 to three tactical fighter wings: the 8th at Ubon, an all-F-4 unit, and the two Thud wings, the 355th and 388th, at Takhli and Korat.

The Thuds had been loaded for anticipated strikes that day with their usual array of six 750 lb M117 bombs and external fuel tanks. When the word came through that the target was the Doumer bridge, it meant that the 750-pounders had to be off-loaded and replaced with 3,000 lb M118 bombs. The planners had learned from the lessons of the attack on the Dragon's Jaw bridge and specified the heavier ordnance. The mission was scheduled to take-off at about 2:00pm, which left little time to change the armament load, a task usually requiring about one hour for each aircraft. By looking the other way in feigned ignorance of established and conservative safe operations, the commanders let their efficient, ingenious, and sweating ground crews get on with the job of servicing their aircraft 'hot', weapons and fuel loaded together. The planes were re-armed in less than one-third of the usual time as the crews worked in the mid-day heat, through lunch break, to get the work done.

Col Robert H. White, a former X-15 research pilot who had qualified for astronaut's wings in that transitional

space ship, was called on to lead the strike. He was Deputy Commander of the 355th TFW, the unit that would be first in on the target. He picked 19 of his most-experienced pilots for the mission and they got to work with the maps, briefings, checkout of personal gear, target photos, and line-up cards with call signs, frequencies and other necessary information. By 1:00pm they were at the flight line, carrying parachutes, loaded pistols and – most importantly – water bottles. A long flight, at high altitude and at midday, is a sure way to dehydrate rapidly and to fall victim to fatigue. Water prevents this.

The pilots were met by the crew chiefs, and the walk-around began. Check the bombs; check the contact fuses; check the safety wires that keep the bombs from detonating before they are dropped. Check the tires, the landing gear, the visible panels, the safety streamers, the covers that should have been removed, pat the belly – or whatever other affectionate act is ritualistically performed by the pilot before a mission – then clamber up the ladder and into the heat-soaked cockpit. The crew chief helps with the harness, checks the oxygen, takes the pins from the ejection seat, wishes you luck, and backs down the ladder.

It is 13.50 hours and you poke the starter button. The cartridge starter fires, its acrid smoke cloud swirling through the revetment. At 8 percent rpm, the J75 is ready to go and you open the throttle while the whine builds to a roar. With power, you taxi out, the Thud waddling and weaving as you head for the runway. At 14.18, Col White and his wingman barrel down the blacktop, their Thuds

ABOVE
Two D-30REs, 62-4244 and -4253, wait for take-off clearance from Kadena AB, Japan. They are attached to the 18th TFW, part of the Pacific Air Forces (PACAF)

RIGHT
Taxiing at Kadena, ready for a practice mission with the six 750 lb bombs slung from the centerline MEWR. A gun pod is on the outboard starboard pylon

in full afterburner and their water-injection systems dumping liquid into the engine. Count 11 seconds; the second element follows White's into the air. Ten times it happens; 20 Thuds position, roll, lift off, start the turn. Two spares trail them, in case there is an abort.

They head north, to rendezvous with the KC-135A tankers from Detachment 1, 4258th Strategic Wing, coming out of U-Tapao, another of the Thai bases. There are Thuds everywhere, armed for their specific missions. Four of them are flying Iron Hand, two are Wild Weasel F-105s and there is a pair of F-105Ds with iron bombs. Four more Ds are armed with cluster bombs for flak suppression. The bombing force carries the paired 3,000-pounders. Some of the F-4s carry bombs, as well, and the remainder of the flight is along for MIGCAP, to keep the interceptors off the Thuds' backs. There are four EB-66Cs for jamming and other devious electronic tricks.

The border with North Vietnam is crossed, and the pilots start 'greening up' their armament switches, setting them for proper release of the bombs and getting the green safe light indications after each set of practised

hand motions. A hundred miles to Hanoi; there's the Red River, and it's time to power up to 0.9 Mach at 10,000 feet. Four minutes to go and the force begins its turn to the south-east and follows the line of hills known as Thud Ridge.

The first MiGs show and blow through the formations in a vain attempt at a head-on intercept. They only get one chance at that shot; if they miss on the first pass, there is no possibility of turning and catching the Thuds for a second. White banks towards the south, and the rest of the force streams behind him, heading straight for the Doumer bridge just visible in the distance.

Time for the pop; the Thuds climb to 13,000 feet, a struggle at their weight. The first flight is ready and White rolls into his bomb run, followed by his wingman and then the second element of two Thuds. Down the chute they speed, afterburners full on, burning fuel at a

hell of a rate and pushing the Thuds into supersonic speed. it's a long 7 seconds; then the bombs drop away, the Thuds jolt upwards, lighter by 3 tons. From 7,000 feet, the bombs hurtle down while the Thuds make the pull-up, turn to follow the river downstream and roar above the Hanoi Hilton still in full afterburner, the howl and the sonic boom sending a morale-boosting message to the airmen imprisoned there.

'Giraffe! Giraffe! Giraffe!

The code is broadcast three times, and back at Takhli and Korat and Ubon they know that the strike has been a success. White's element has hit and dropped one span, flight two and three have dropped two more. One of the flak batteries has been smashed; the other survives, badly damaged. Two SAM sites no longer exist, and none of the others has managed to launch a good shot, because the defense-suppression flight has kept them out of action.

Photographed before mid-1965, when camouflage paint was decreed, this New Jersey ANG F-105RE, 57-5804, is gleaming in its aluminized lacquer finish. The weapon load is a typical 14 750 lb bombs on the centerline MER and inboard pylons, and at least one Bullpup A on the outboard

The bridge and its underpinnings have been rocked by 94 tons of bombs; three spans are in the river. Two Thuds have been hit, but their pilots have nursed them back to safe landings.

The post-strike assessment, from photos taken by a daring RF-4C who flashed over the site a few seconds after the last bomber had gone, showed one rail span and two highway spans in the water. The north highway approach was cut. The loads of 26 trains a day – about 6,000 tons of supplies – would have to be moved into Hanoi by some other means. It was a good strike, but the North Vietnamese were as resilient as the Thuds had been unrelenting. By 3 October the bridge was open for traffic again.

After three more strikes, another bridge was begun downstream, bypassing the Doumer and serving as an alternative for rail traffic. By the end of the 1967 Rolling

A New Jersey ANG Thud touches down on the wet runway at
Seymour Johnson AFB, North Carolina

Thunder campaign, the bridge had been attacked by 177
bombers – most of them Thuds – which had dumped 380
tons of bombs. By then, it was being defended by more
than 300 AAA batteries, 84 SAM sites with four to six
missile launchers at each site and a couple of dozen MiG
interceptors. The USAF lost two aircraft to flak and
another 15 were damaged during the attacks. Meanwhile,
Paul Doumer's monument still stood.

By then, the war was inevitably winding down for the
Thud. Its losses in combat were reducing the force to a
minimum; the wings at Korat and Takhli were down to
three squadrons, instead of four. During the 1965, more
than 60 F-105s had been lost to the enemy and in 1966
the figure jumped to 85. After the attack on the Doumer
bridge, the subsequent interdiction campaigns and
bombing raids up north cost the Thuds heavily. In
October 1967, 14 more were gone and in November, 16.
Some of the pilots with a macabre sense of humor were
able to show, by statistics, that it would be impossible to
complete the tour of 100 combat missions without being
downed.

The last Thud had been delivered in January 1965, the
production line shut down and the tools placed in long-
term storage. It was a pity, because the Thud was such a
fine aircraft for the job. Pilots loved it; it took them home
time after time, when the flak or a near-miss by a SAM
had torn holes in primary structure and left raw and
jagged chunks of metal bent back by the breeze.

One Thud on a mission up north was hit by anti-
aircraft fire, which severed the entire right side of the

ABOVE
The Air Force Reserve unit at Hill AFB, Utah, flew a mix of
F-105B and D models. Shown is 62-4318, a D-31RE

BELOW
One of the least-publicized bi-centennial color schemes was
this, on F-105B-10RE, 57-5776, from the New Jersey ANG.
The tail fin was a light blue, with a red-and-white striped rudder

stabilator. That Thud, aided by some superb piloting,
came back 300 miles to a friendly base and a safe landing.

Another F-105D, piloted by Maj William McClelland,
flew a mission against a highway bridge across the Kinh
Bich Dong river. As he pulled out of his bomb run, his
plane was hammered by an 85mm shell. This hit the right
inboard pylon, which normally held a 450-gallon fuel
tank, and exploded, tearing laterally through the wing,
parallel to the main spar, leaving a substantial portion of
the wing structure standing out perpendicular to the wing
surface. Remarkably McClelland was able to trim out the
extra drag and to fly his mangled Thud back to base.

Capt Donald L. Hodge, leading a strike against a river
ferry and its piers, was still in his bomb run, starting the
pull-up after release, when his Thud was struck by a
57mm shell. 'The first indication I had of the hit,' he
said, 'was when about 6 feet of the leading edge of my left
wing disappeared.' The shell kept ploughing through the
structure, finishing in the nose where it exploded, the
blast wrecking Hodge's radar and bulging the nose
panels. The Thud then took a second hit from the 57mm
battery, this time on an underwing bomb pylon. The
shell tore through and exploded under the cockpit,
bouncing Hodge's feet off the floor and tearing some 50
holes in the fuselage sides. 'I knew the aircraft was heavily
damaged because it didn't have much speed and was hard

The 466th TFS, 419th TFW, at Hill operated the high-time Thud, an F-105D-31RE, 62-4347, with more than 6,900 hours of logged flight time. The MER is carrying two practice bombs with spotting charges

to handle. I didn't really know how bad it was until I landed, and they hooked a tug to it and towed it off,' said Hodge later.

It was accepted fact that the Thud was rugged, but how rugged was a question that hadn't been answered exactly. One of the ways of getting an answer was designed by some inquisitive AFLC engineers. They instrumented six Thuds at Takhli and six at Korat with equipment to measure the g loads during flight, the static pressure and the dynamic pressure as functions of elapsed flight time. The resulting traces could be related to air-speed and – when interpreted – would produce data about the frequency and the intensity of air loads imposed during combat.

Of the dozen aircraft they chose to instrument, four soon crashed, two were damaged and four became unavailable because of requirements for extended maintenance. Seven additional Thuds were then instrumented to produce enough data to draw valid conclusions. Between 14 August 1966 and 29 April 1967, 3,055 hours of combat time were recorded. The Thuds were commonly flying at take-off weights between 49,500 and 50,900 pounds. They were loaded with six M117 bombs on a centerline multiple stores rack and with 450-gallon external fuel tanks on both inboard pylons.

What the engineers found was probably not too surprising, although the actual magnitude of the loads was. They discovered that combat loads were higher than non-combat, but that was not news. However, the combat loads were higher than the design loads, meaning that the aircraft was being subjected routinely to stresses for

which it had not been built, even though it had been designed for $8.67g$ in subsonic maneuvering and $7.33g$ in supersonic.

The maximum recorded combat load was an equivalent of $10.3g$, achieved in supersonic flight. The aircraft was one of the F-105Ds out of Korat and it was on a bombing mission. It experienced that load while it was at an altitude of 7,811 feet and an air-speed of 587 knots, equivalent to Mach 1.02. The airplane weighed 41,598 pounds, approximately, at the instant of the loading. Since that altitude is typical of a bomb-release height, it is likely that the pilot had just released his ordnance and was making a pull-out from the run.

Korat F-105s were apparently flown by a hardy breed of pilots (those who operated out of Takhli would probably have referred to the Korat crew as 'heavy-handed'). The Thud pilots of the 388th TFW flew eight out of the eleven aircraft, and produced peak combat loads above $7.5g$. One of the Korat F-105Ds – serial number 62-4352 – exceeded $7.5g$ 89 times during 1,000 flight hours, which was almost three times as much as the next nearest over-stressing of 31 times. As expected, the maximum peak loads occurred during manoeuvering flight, but quite surprisingly, the Korat aircraft were frequently loaded to as high as $6.5g$ during let-down to base.

Republic field service representatives remember the F-105 as the finest flying machine available, but point out that maintenance was very tedious and that neither was the aircraft easy to fix. The average break rate, one said, was 50 percent, but that was mostly due to avionic systems and equipment. Part of the blame must be placed on Kartveli, a designer obsessed with cleanliness of lines and smoothness of structure. He hated access panels, hated to disrupt the sleek contours of his elegant aircraft.

Technicians remember a classic example: the way they had to replace a back-up inverter, a part of the electrical system which often developed trouble. It was located in a compartment under the pilot's seat, a place that, in any other plane, would be accessible from the outside through removable panels. Not so in Kartveli's F-105; to get at that inverter, ground crews had to remove the pilot's seat and rudder pedals. Said one, 'You had to yank out half the cockpit to get to that damned inverter.'

The heat and humidity of Thailand were no help. Condensation seeped in everywhere, regardless of paint, covers and other protection. Typically, it would get into the AC control panel, and could cause real damage there.

That's not exactly an approved use of the crew boarding ladder, but you improvise in this business. A technician checks out some semi-hidden item on 62-4383, an F-105D-31RE from the 419th TFW at Hill AFB

Once the cure was discovered, however – a few minutes of hot air blasting from an external power unit universally called the Dash 60 – it was a problem which was easily solved.

The F-105D had a very high operational availability in south-east Asia, with the NORS (not operationally ready, spares) down around 7 or 8 percent on any day. The Air Force goal for its entire force was 5 percent. The 388th TFW at Korat achieved a remarkable record during the summer of 1967, when it established a 99.77 percent take-off rate (0.23 abort rate) during one month. The 355th, during the same summer, had one F-105D which logged 153.2 flight hours during one month, a new mark for the theater.

During the following summer, the 388th established another exceptional mark, when its NORS rate varied between zero and 0.4 percent. The wing averaged about 70 hours on each aircraft in each month of that summer and kept the abort rate down below 1 percent, once dipping to a value of 0.4.

Part of the reason for such availability was that it was wartime, and so maintenance units were manned at 125 percent of normal requirements. Further, ground crews worked three shifts, around the clock. Thus, there was enough manpower available to do a complete periodic or phase inspection overnight. There were plenty of spares in the pipeline from the Sacramento Air Materiel Area, so a minimum of cannibalization was necessary.

The situation was further eased by the ready availability of RAM (Rapid Aircraft Maintenance) teams. These were specialized groups of military and civilian personnel – generally numbering 18 men – from repair depots, who were particularly skilled in repairing battle – or crash-damaged aircraft. The first one was sent to Thailand in April 1965 to repair two F-105s after they had crashed.

Another reason for the high availability was that the pilots did not write up all the squawks they had about an aircraft. They concentrated on the ones that affected its ability to fly and its safety margins and let the others go until a more-convenient time.

The J75 engines were severely stressed, especially in the hot sections. The powerplants had a reputation for ruggedness and the pilots did not baby them. When they neared the target areas, they shoved throttles through the gate into full afterburner operation and kept them there until they were safely on the way home. So the demand for spare parts in the hot section was high and occasionally shortages developed. The engines were changed every 125 hours routinely, instead of at the established Air Force mark of 200.

The theorectical fatigue life of the F-105 had been calculated at 4,000 flight hours. Normally, fatigue calculations are made with an awareness of the possibility of a large scatter in the results. Consequently, specifying

RIGHT
The afterburner kicks in with a thunderclap, and the heavy Thud begins its take-off roll. This F-105D-31RE (62-4348) is part of the 465th TFS, 419th TFW, and based at Tinker AFB, Oklahoma

BELOW
A lineup of D model Thuds of the 465th TFS at Tinker AFB, Oklahoma

This F-105G Wild Weasel, 62-4416, carries a rocket launcher
on the centerline pylon. The aircraft is from the 562nd TFS,
35th TFW at George AFB, California

RIGHT
What's wrong with this Thud? Check the tail number; it
belongs to 63-8362, an F-105F-1RE. But the tail is attached to a
single-seat D model, serial unknown. The Virginia ANG moves
in mysterious ways

a 4,000-hour safe life could mean that many aircraft
might easily live to 5,000, 6,000 or even more hours,
while a few would start to show their age close to the
4,000-hour mark. By May 1967, many of the F-105s in
service had logged more than 1,500 hours. The first
F-105D to top the 2,000-hour level flew with the 354th
TFS at Takhli and by September 1968, one F-105D, in
combat since August 1966, had more than 3,000 hours in
its log and had flown more than 500 mission up north.
This was F-105D 60-0428. The first to reach the
theorectical fatigue life limit of 4,000 hours was 'Honey
Pot II', an F-105D 61-0159, with more than 600 combat
missions and one MiG kill to her credit.

Pilots were expected to fly 100 missions over North
Vietnam to complete a single tour of combat duty and
missions over Laos, however numerous or risky, did not
count towards the total. The average pilot completed his
tour in about seven months and logged approximately
300 hours of combat time during that period. In 1966, the
355th TFW showed a total of 45,810 flight hours on
combat missions, while in early 1967, the wing increased
that figure to 4,500 a month. One of its F-105Ds was
flown for more than 132 hours during one month in early
1967.

On 31 March 1968, a halt in the bombing of the north,
was called by President Lyndon B. Johnson, a halt which

was to last four years. During the halt, the need for deep interdiction by tactical strike aircraft lessened. The long-range, high-speed, load-carrying capability of the F-105s was more than was required in the theater and so units were sent back to the United States and by October 1969, the 388th TFW was down to a single squadron, the 44th TFS, and that unit left Korat – its long-time home base – to fly the short distance to Takhli, where it became a part of the 355th TFW.

The bombing halt ended abruptly when troops of North Vietnam invaded the south on 30 March 1972. On 6 April, American air strikes against targets north of the demilitarized zone were resumed, but by that time the USAF order of battle included only 16 F-105s, all at Korat, a mere 4 percent of the total of 365 strike aircraft. The Thud had been replaced by Phantoms.

The remainder of the available, and surviving, F-105s were in service in the United States and the need for more fighters of all types was met by the Constant Guard I deployment, which moved units from CONUS to SEA. This deployment included a dozen F-105G Wild Weasels from the 561st TFS at McConnell. They left on 7 April

ABOVE & BELOW
On 25 May 1983 the last Thud in the Air National Guard, an F-105F-1RE, 63-8299, retired with with an official final flight. The symbol of 19 years F-105 service in the Guard, and on the roster of the Georgia ANG's 128th TFS, 116th TFW and appropriately decorated for the last flight. Its call sign was Peach 91, so a Georgia peach was painted between the cockpits. On the left wing tank, letters on a red, white and blue ribbon stated 'Thunderchief'; on the right, 'Thuds Forever'. On the upper right wing panel, large letters proclaimed the 116th TFW

and the first one arrived at Korat on 12 April to begin flying combat missions on that day.

On 30 May, the order of battle reflected the presence of 31 F-105s at Korat, out of a total strike force of 501 aircraft. There were still F-105Gs at Korat more than two years later, serving with the 17th WWS, operating at a authorized strength of 18 aircraft. The unit was finally deployed back to CONUS and the very last F-105G left south-east Asia on 29 October 1974, concluding a nine-year presence in Thailand.

As the Thunderchiefs left the battle zones for the relative quiet of the mainland bases, they were parcelled out to Air National Guard (ANG) and Air Force Reserve (AFRES) units.

When the 355th TFW returned from Takhli to McConnell AFB, Kansas, in 1970, it was absorbed by the 23rd TFW until its assets – a somehow cold and distant way to refer to aircraft with such vitality – could be

disposed to the ANG units.

The 23rd TFW at that time included two training squadrons, the 562nd and 563rd, which taught pilots how to fly the F-105. Students completed a six-week curriculum which included about 125 hours of classroom time, 8 hours in the simulator, about 24 hours of flying time and another 24 hours with a field training detachment. The training task was later turned over to the 184th Tactical Fighter Training Group of the Kansas ANG, also based at McConnell, which became the last unit charged with the mission of training F-105 pilots. The 184th was equipped with 18 F-105s which had returned from combat.

Additionally, ANG units in New Jersey, Washington DC, and Virginia, the AFRES 301st TFG at Carswell AFB, Texas, the 507th TFG at Tinker AFB, Oklahoma, and the 508th TFG at Hill AFB, Utah, were among those units which operated the F-105s post-war with considerable success. The Thunderstick II Thuds went to the 457th TFS, 301st TFG. That unit had been re-activated in the Reserve in July 1972 and operated the T-stick II Thuds under a mission statement calling for precision bombing. By March 1982, most of the T-stick II Thuds had been ferried to MASDC and cocooned. The straight D models from the 457th TFS had been ferried to the 466th TFS, 508th TFG.

The 466th TFS was in the spring of 1983 the sole surviving F-105 unit anywhere; it was formed in January

1973 to fly the F-105B model and became combat-ready in September of that year, a record time of eight months. In January 1980, the unit converted to the D/F models, while on 1 October 1982 the 508th TFG, parent organization to the 466th TFS, was de-activated and the 419th TFW was formed, with subordinate units including the 466th TFS and the 507th TFG at Tinker AFB.

Post-war service in CONUS

The 17th WWS was de-activated during 1974 at George AFB, California, and its aircraft and other equipment were taken over by the newly formed 562nd

RIGHT
Some of the awesome sound, heat and power of a Thud take-off is captured in this shot of an F-105F of the Georgia ANG. The centerline MER holds small practice bombs

BELOW
Another view of the Georgia ANGs, F-105F-1RE, Peach 91

BELOW LEFT
F-105F-1RE, 62-4417, the sixth two-seat Thud built, sits on the ramp next to a Canadian Armed Forces CF-101, the design against which the Thud competed fiercely and effectively

TFS of the 35th TFW at George (that squadron and its sister 561st were earlier part of the 23rd TFW at McDonnell). The 35th was already operating one squadron of F-105G Wild Weasels; its 561st TFS had returned to the US from Thailand almost a year before the 17th pulled up stakes. It was assigned to the 35th in the autumn of 1973, after a term with the 23rd TFW. Those two complete F-105G squadrons, plus the 563rd Tactical Fighter Training Squadron – which operated a mix of F-105Gs and F-4Cs for training Wild Weasel aircrews – represented the last presence of the Thunderchief with operational squadrons of the USAF. Their phase-out began on 28 April 1978, when the first of the F-4G Wild Weasel aircraft was accepted by Tactical Air Command.

The Wild Weasel aircraft at George were then divided between the 128th TFS of the 116th TFW, Georgia Air National Guard, and the Military Aircraft Storage and Disposition Center (MASDC), at Davis-Monthan AFB, Arizona. With the planes that went to Georgia went part of the Wild Weasel mission, and the 128th TFS began its conversion from the F-100 to the F-105G on 1 January 1979.

The Georgia ANG converted under TAC's Ready TEAM (Tactical Enhancement and Modernization) plan, a scheduled change which had as a broad goal the maintenance of a maximum force of combat-ready aircraft. The 128th was scheduled to complete its conversion in 270 days after its official start and had to maintain a combat-ready status on its F-100s while in that conversion.

The Guard moved fast, partially because both Guard and Reserve units have personnel – both pilots and technicians – who are much more experienced than the personnel in the regular Air Force. By March 1979, the 128th was able to deploy five F-105Gs on a Red Flag exercise at Nellis AFB, and by June it had eight mission-ready aircrews out of the 11 assigned, seven mission-ready aircrews out of 20 formed and seven pilots and 11 EWOs qualified as mission-ready.

Training was handicapped by the lack of a local electronic warfare range for practice sorties; so the 128th improvised and went where the action was, participating in every available exercise where threat signals were generated. Further, the Georgia ANG devised its own composite strike exercise and arranged for the Navy to provide simulated threat signals from destroyers and fast frigates. The 128th deployed to the electronic warfare ranges in the area around Eglin and MacDill AFB, Florida, then salvaged a couple of threat emitters from

ABOVE LEFT
On the glide path and a half-mile out, this Thud driver is set to land on the long runway at McConnell AFB, Kansas

LEFT
In the latter days of the Thud, training programs were assigned to the Kansas ANG 184th TFTG, McConnell AFB, Wichita, Kansas. This is one of their F-105Fs, 63-8294, taxiing out for a practice bombing mission

The 562nd TFS of the 23rd TFW, training replacement crews in the Thud at McConnell AFB, Kansas, included this elegant F model, 63-8300, among its equipment

ABOVE & BELOW
Two more views of Thunderchief F-105F, 63-8300, based at
McConnell AFB, Kansas, with the 562nd TFS of the 23rd
TFW

military junkyards and made its own simulated SAM
radars for operational use in local exercises.

The state of the F-105G aircraft was, as can be
imagined, poor. They had been through a war and service
with a training squadron and were nearing the end of
their useful lives. The 116th TFW, the parent
organization, developed, proposed and received approval
to modify the Weasel Thuds and the changes thus made
reduced weight and drag and consumption by about 100
gallons per hour of flying time.

Between mid 1980 and mid 1981, the 128th began to
experience major problems with its fleet of F-105Gs. The
aircraft were delivered late, reflecting equally late
deliveries of the F-4G to the units re-equipping at George
AFB. On top of this, the Gs developed fuel cell problems
and the 116th TFW installations at Dobbins AFB –
although modern and well equipped – did not have a
specialized fuel-cell repair facility. So the maintenance
crews improvised; they replaced 55 cells, and changed
the fire-suppressant foam in 155 more, a tedious and
difficult job under any circumstances. Then they had to
remove and inspect engine combustion chamber cases;
more than half of them were found to be cracked and had
to be replaced. The ground crews rewired 20 wings, 10
instrument panels and six fuselage aft sections, and

repaired eight fuel-cell cavities that had corroded.

By July 1981, the situation was serious. The 128th TFS had three flyable aircraft left after the engine combustion cases had been inspected; out of the 34 engines the unit had, 31 needed repairs. What made it worse was that 33 replacement parts from the pipeline were defective and useless. Then another inspection discovered that some main landing gear side braces were cracked. For these parts, there were no replacements, so they had to be salvaged from the aircraft in storage at MASDC. And when those finally arrived, half of them were also cracked and useless. More cracks were then found in the wing spars and other wing locations.

In spite of this pyramid of problems, the maintenance people of 116th TFW achieved an absolutely remarkable feat. They increased the flyable fleet from three to just over half the establishment strength of 24 aircraft. They reduced maintenance man-hours per sortie from a high of 90·2 to a level of 58·1. The air abort rate was 0·3 percent and the ground abort rate was 2·1 percent. While they were doing this, the wing was working on a major

modification to load the Standard ARM missile on the fuselage centerline station, instead of on a wing pylon. It was accomplished in time to deploy aircraft to a Red Flag exercise with the new installations. The advantages of the new installation included increased safety of operations and considerable fuel savings because of reduced installation drag.

Even further, the 128th participated in 17 exercises during the year ending 30 June 1982, eight of them requiring unit deployments. One of them was a two-week Red Flag/Green Flag TAC exercise emphasizing electronic welfare; another was a five-day deployment, during which the pilots fired 19 live Shrike missiles on an instrumented range. And to top it off, they completed nine years of accident-free flying, of which the more recent had been with an aircraft forecast to have the third highest accident rate in the USAF. In language best understood by those who have been there, the performance of the ground and flying personnel of the 116th TFW, Georgia Air National Guard, was truly Sierra Hotel.

8
Lightning Bolts

The Thunderchief was born to carry a nuclear weapon to a distant target. It was conceived during the era of massive retaliation, of unimaginable sunbursts of radiation and heat, of the horrendous beauty of the radioactive pillar of cloud by day and a pillar of fire by night. Strategists and tacticians spoke of the use of nuclear weapons as casually as they had talked, a few years earlier, of the dropping of high explosives on Germany and fire bombs on Japan. Nuclear bombs were just another type of weapon, that's all, to be delivered by strategic and tactical bombers, hurled through space in missile warheads or blasted into enemy territory from artillery or battlefield rockets.

Deep within the metallic bowels of the F-105 lay a secret cavern, a space menacing when empty and terrifying when filled. It was the reason for being of the Thunderchief, a bomb bay that was 190 inches (15ft 10in) long, 32 inches wide, and 32 inches high. The bay was covered by two doors which met at the bottom centerline of the fuselage, and retracted inside the fuselage, to minimize their drag contribution.

In other references to the F-105, it is said that its bomb bay was the size of that of the famed Boeing B-17 Fortress of World War II, but this is untrue. The Fortress' bay was only about 8 feet long – much shorter than the F-105's – but it was also about 6 feet wide and the same dimension high, more than twice the equivalent measurements of the F-105. Bomb *loads* are something else. The F-105 could, but didn't very often, carry as much of a bomb load, measured in pounds, as did the B-17 or the Consolidated B-24 Liberator.

The size of the F-105 bomb bay was determined by the bulk of the nuclear weapons of the day. By the time the Thunderchief was in service, the design technology of nuclear weaponry had produced a range of bombs of

With 12 MK-82 500 lb bombs slung under its wings, F-105B, FH-836 slices through cumulus clouds on a test mission out of Eglin AFB

several shapes and yields, capable of being dropped in free-fall ballistic trajectory or in a free flight retarded by a drag chute and of being carried inside a bomb bay or outside on wing or fuselage pylons.

The F-105 was designed to carry at least five, and perhaps six, different nuclear weapons, internally or externally. In the following listing, their yields are given in megatons or kilotons, the standard method of describing nuclear explosive power. A one-kiloton yield is an explosive power equal to that of 1,000 tons of TNT; a one-megaton yield is equivalent to the explosive power of 1,000,000 tons of TNT.

Mk-7, one of the earliest atomic bombs, was designated as one of two alternative payloads in the first detail specification for the F-105. It weighed 1,677·8lb, according to the F-105 spec weight statement, but was always referred to as a '1,700lb store'. Its yield was, according to one source, in the kiloton range; a meaningless figure, but one probably intended to compare it to a Hiroshima strength weapon. It

was encased in a streamlined housing 15ft 5in long, with a 30in diameter. Three fins, arranged 120-degrees apart with the lower one vertical, provided stability. The lower fin could be retracted for fighter installations. It was designed to be detonated either in the air or on the ground following a laydown delivery.

USAF 'bluff shape', not further identified, was the other bomb load designated by the original F-105 specification. Its dimensions correspond to those of the Mk-43 weapon described below, so the 'bluff shape' may have been an early configuration or a development stage on the way to the final Mk-43 streamlined bomb. Dimensions cited were a length of 13ft 8½in, a diameter of 18in and a weight of 2,000lb. Yield was quoted as one megaton.

Mk-28, one of the oldest thermo-nuclear systems, could be assembled in five different configurations, with yields controllable between 1.1 and 20 megatons (making it between 80 and 1,400 times as powerful as Little Boy). Depending on the chosen yield, it could vary in length between 9 and 14ft. Its diameter was 20in. The weight

ABOVE
Close-up of the MN-1/A practice special weapons dispenser

ABOVE LEFT
F-105Ds were assigned to the AF Armament Center, Eglin AFB, Florida, for tests on a wide variety of weapons. One was the MK-28 nuclear store, shown here in one of its five possible assemblies on 58-1149, the fourth F-105D-1RE

LEFT
FH-149, carrying a BDU-8/B, shows the special target markings used to establish space position from phototheodolite sightings made during flight tests

varied with the yield. It could be dropped in free-fall, or retarded by a drag parachute and would normally have been carried externally.

Mk-43, also a thermo-nuclear weapon, was designed for internal or external carriage on a number of fighter-bombers. Its yield was approximately one megaton. It was about 13ft 9in long and 18in in maximum diameter and was housed in a streamlined casing. Its total weight was about 1 ton. It could be dropped either in free-fall or retarded mode.

Mk-57, a relatively low-yield (15-20 kilotons) thermo-nuclear weapon, could be carried either externally or internally on the F-105. It was a little under 10ft long, and about 15in in maximum diameter. Both the Mk-43 and Mk-57 weapons were developed during the early 1960s at the Los Alamos Scientific Laboratory, New Mexico.

Mk-61, a thermo-nuclear weapon, had a yield of between 100 and 500 kilotons. It was 11ft 9in long and had a 13in casing diameter and was normally dropped with a retarding chute. It could be carried externally on the F-105.

The F-105B model was designated to be able to load, as its usual nuclear ordnance, three Mk-38 bombs, one Mk-43, or three Mk-61 bombs. The D model was capable of loading four Mk-28 or Mk-43 weapons, one Mk-57 or one Mk-61. The F-105F could handle four of either the Mk-28 or Mk-43, three of the Mk-61 types or one the Mk-57.

Both the F-105D and F-105F models demonstrated enormous carrying capacity with conventional ordnance. Both models had 17 fuselage and wing stations to which external stores could be attached and both were cleared to carry routinely a maximum weapons load of 7 tons (their contemporaries in Vietnam, the F-4C and F-4D, carried $4\frac{1}{2}$ tons on ground-attack missions).

Three types of conventional high-explosive general-purpose bombs (generally referred to as 'iron' bombs or,

as laser-guided 'smart' bombs came along later, 'dumb' bombs) were the usually components of F-105 ordnance for the journey northward:

M117 750lb bomb, actually weighing 823!b, with a cast-steel case contained 403lb of Minol 2 or Tritonal;
Mk-83 1,000lb bomb, at 985lb with 445 pounds of Minol 2, Tritonal, or H6, housed in a cast-steel case;
M118 3,000lb bomb, loaded with 1,975lb of Tritonal in a cast-steel casing and weighing 3049lb.

One of the persistent problems with dropping bombs

BELOW LEFT
This centerline store is a BDU-12/B, similar geometrically to the BDU-8/B but containing a different load of weaponry

BELOW RIGHT
Described as an MD-6, the shape is characteristic of the nuclear weapons. On the pylon, just above the figures 58-11, is marked MK-28/43, the designations of two nuclear stores cleared for the F-105D

BELOW
FH-774, an F-105D-6RE, 59-1774, stands on the ramp at Eglin with a load of BLU-1/B fire bombs.

from aircraft is getting them to drop. There have been cases where bombs were released, then stayed in free flight inside the bomb bay, moving ominously from side to side in an erratic motion. Bombs have been dropped, have fallen just below the bomb bay and been mysteriously propelled back into the bomb bay. Bombs have tumbled dangerously, become violently unstable and in general performed as unpredictably as imaginable. The danger is obvious; once released, a bomb starts to arm itself. The air-driven propellers which activate the fuses operate and within a few seconds the bomb is ready to be detonated. Unstable bombs, salvoed in an

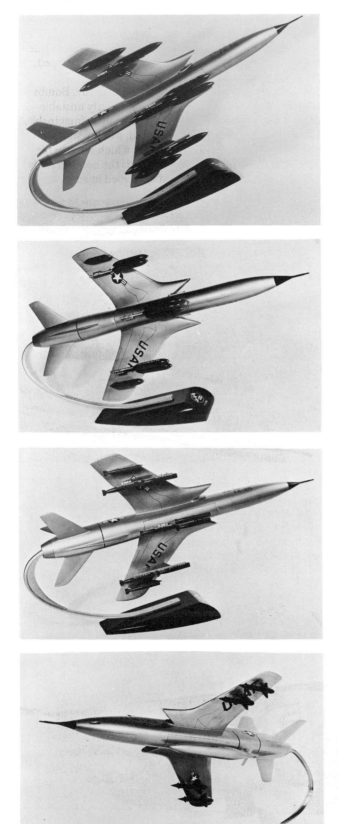

ABOVE
Bullpup missiles were carried on the outboard pylons, with the inboards reserved for fuel. Here, FH-459 a D-10RE, shows the arrangement

LEFT, TOP TO BOTTOM
This models shows nine fire bombs on the wing and fuselage racks

Another standard armament arrangement for the F-105D was an array of nine LAU-3/A or LAU-18 rocket pods

A study model shows the proposed carriage of nine MLU-10/B mines

The Thud could carry four GAM-A or B Bullpup missiles, and a 650-gallon tank on the centerline

emergency, have collided, detonated and destroyed the carrier aircraft. At best the recalcitrant may only batter some of the bomb bay structure; at worst, it may blow up the entire contents of the bomb bay and the aircraft.

The original bomb bay design, said one Republic engineer, used a swinging arm system which moved the bomb physically down out of the bay before releasing it. That was not satisfactory, and eventually it was replaced – before the Thunderchief went into production – by an ejection mechanism. George Hildebrand, the engineer who designed it, had been sitting and staring at his drawing board, idly doodling. He pressed the top of the pencil to extend more lead; the jaws of the mechanical pinch chuck expanded, and moved further out, ejecting the lead cleanly and swiftly – and of such simple actions are design ideas born. The pencil was reassembled, and

put to work sketching an ejection mechanism which would clamp on to the bomb fittings and expel them forcibly when actuated for release, pushing the bomb out of the bomb bay with a substantially initial velocity.

Republic and the Air Force were concerned about the ejection and drop characteristics of some of the strange shapes seen in new weapons designs and requested a series of wind-tunnel tests which might quell their fears. NACA developed an extensive and continuing program of model tests which simulated full-scale drops from the bomb bay. The models were tested in the 27 × 27in pre-flight jet of the Langley Pilotless Aircraft Research Station at Wallops Island, Virginia. At least 15 shapes were tested, and the results were used to recommend the optimum operational designs and methods of ejection and release.

LEFT
This closeup of a Bullpup on the outboard pylon shows the missiles forward steering vanes and the small clearances between its fins and the pylon mounting

BELOW LEFT
FH-836 at Eglin, and another arrangement of 500 lb MK-82 bombs. It seems to be carrying 26: Four racks, each with six, and one on each outboard pylon. But officially, the maximum load was 16 of the 500 lb weapons

BELOW
The airman, pulling the last of the safety lock pins, gives scale to the immense size of the Thud. The load is six 750 lb M117 bombs

The background to these tests was a 1953 NACA report of wind-tunnel tests simulating bomb drops at supersonic speeds. The results showed that '...serious troubles may be encountered.' One of the first tests was made on the Mk-7 store, which required folding fins – a Republic modification to the basic design of the casing – in order to fit in the bomb bay of the F-105. The fins opened only after the store was ejected and it was suspected that the time lag between release and fin opening could have a major effect on the stability of the weapon.

Tests in the pre-flight jet, simulating subsonic and supersonic (Mach 1.4) release of the Mk-7 at 3,400ft and supersonic (Mach 1.4 and 1.98) release at 29,000ft confirmed the problem. At low altitude and supersonic speed – one design point for the F-105 – the streamlined shape of the store slammed into the bomb bay and fuselage after release. NACA recommended that a larger fin with lower aspect ration be designed to replace the original fin assembly, that supersonic releases be made only at higher altitudes and that the fins should snap open in four milliseconds to achieve the desired flight stability.

The tests gradually narrowed down the choices of desirable shapes and – as one result – a family of so-called 'bluff shapes' was designed for nuclear weapons intended for internal carriage. The F-105 was known, of course, for its ability to carry about anything that the Air Force or the Navy had developed in the way of bombs and external stores.

Sometimes neither a missile nor a bomb could be as effective as a short burst from the Thunderchief's M61 (its earlier designation was T-171E3) 20mm automatic cannon. That weapon – as with most cannon – could be fired during high-*g* manoeuvering combat, something that could not be done with the air-to-air missiles of that day. A competent pilot could 'walk' a burst of 20mm fire through a convoy or a supply train and destroy or severely damage several vehicles.

The M61 was the General Electric Vulcan, a design inspired by the century-old Gatling gun with its rotating barrels. No Gatling, however, could possibly approach the M61 rate of fire, a staggering 6,000 rounds per minute. The cannon had six barrels, weighed 275lb, was hydraulically driven and fired through a blast port and tube on the left side of the F-105 nose. Muzzle velocity was 3,380 feet per second (incidentally, one of the recognition features distinguishing the F-105B from the D was the apparent relative location and shape of that gun port). The kinetic energy in a short burst from the M61 was enough to hammer most ground targets into shards or to saw through an enemy aircraft.

The original specification for the F-105 called for a

ABOVE
Two M118 3,000 lb bombs hang from the inboard pylons of this Thud, on the taxiway at Farmingdale

RIGHT
This is the standard publicity shot for a new fighter-bomber, with all the stores and weapons it can carry laid out in some attractive shape on the ground

quantity of 1,130 20mm M-50 series electrically primed shells as the standard ammunition loading. Later Republic publications describing the armament systems call for a quantity of '...approximately 1,028 rounds.' Either load furnished about 11 seconds of firepower, and the pilots were taught not to hold the trigger down too long.

Republic armament engineers developed two different feed systems for the cannon. For the earlier B model, they designed a dual-feed system, with two feed chutes guiding the 20mm shells into the breech. The links and empty shells were retained after firing, and were stored in

FH-173 banks away to reveal 16, the maximum number of 750
lb M117 bombs that could be carried by a Thunderchief. The
total weight is 13,168 pounds

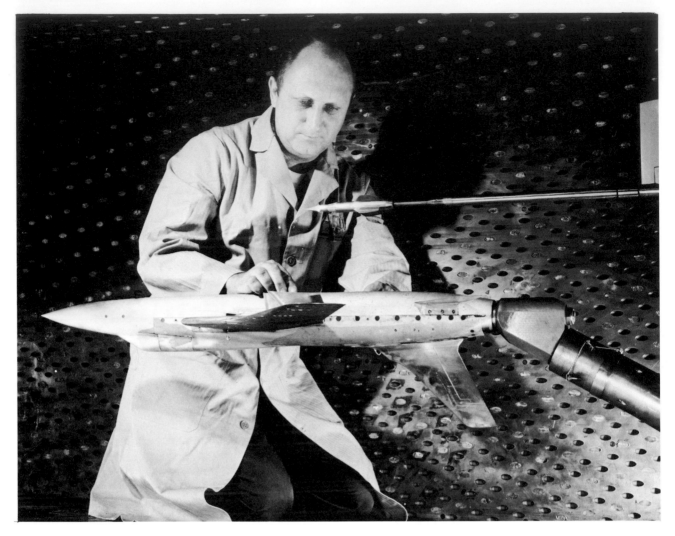

separate compartments. The reason for that arrangement was to minimize the effect of firing on center-of-gravity position. The gun could easily dispose of about 500lb of shells in a short time and that weight shift, so distant from the normal position of the centre of gravity, could cause a significant shift in that point, affecting the aircraft's trim and stability.

The D model required additional space in the nose for the radar system and the only candidate volume was being used for the collection of the links and shells, so the armament engineers redesigned the feed system, removed the empty shell and link retainer compartments and specified a linkless belt to move the shells from their storage drum on to a conveyor which fed them into the breech. Empties were extracted from the breech, relinked on to a second conveyor, and fed back into the drum for storage. The space saved was about 16 cubic feet, enough to house the new radar.

The F-105 was designed at the start of what promised to be the guided-missile age, but its original armament system consisted only of the fixed 20mm cannon, with provisions for carrying external LAU-series pods loaded with 2.75in folding-fin unguided rockets. The specification called for pods on the fuselage centerline

Thunderchief and Bullpup models were tested in a high-speed wind tunnel at the USAF Arnold Engineering Development Center to determine the characteristics of separation

and on both inboard and outboard wing pylons. Armament brochures show the pods and they were cleared for operational use in a series of armament tests, but there is little record of the use of those unguided rockets in the later combat deployment of the F-105D or F. One reference states that the first use of the rocket pods against enemy targets occurred in mid 1968, during the Vietnam war. It further reported that the rockets proved effective against supply and transport targets – meaning, most probably, trucks – in a low-threat area where the Thuds could make a straight-in, close approach without the need to keep jinking in evasive action. That report carried an implication that the accuracy of those folding-fin rockets was pretty poor, which is undoubtedly the reason that they were so little used in the real world of manoeuvering combat.

Missile installation was an inevitable development and the Thunderchief was eventually cleared for a number of them. The first of these systems was a quartette of air-to-air GAR-8 (later to be redesignated AIM-9) Sidewinder

A twin Sidewinder mount was devised and tested on JF-3, 54-0112, during the early days of the Thud program. Thuds went to war with a single Sidewinder installation on each wing

missiles mounted on a double launcher on each outboard wing pylon (at wing station 170, which means that the pylon was located 170 inches from the centerline of the aircraft). Sidewinder models most commonly loaded in Vietnam were the AIM-9B, with passive infra-red guidance systems. They could strike out just beyond 2 miles, reaching a top speed of Mach 2.5 during their flight. Their target-acquisition angle was 25 degrees; any heat source within that cone could be tracked and locked on, while the missile was captive on the carrier aircraft. Sidewinders weighed about 150 pounds and were built by Raytheon and by Ford Aeronutronic.

The F-105D-10RE and later production aircraft were capable of carrying a pair of GAM-83 (later redesignated AGM-12) Bullpup missiles for attacking point ground targets. This first application cleared the Bullpup only for the outboard pylons; on the D-20RE and subsequent aircraft the Bullpup could be carried on both the inboard (at wing Station 129) and outboard pylons. The problem with Bullpup was its radio command guidance, which

required that the pilot maintain line-of-sight with the launched missile until impact (no pilot really liked to hang around a well defended bridge at which he had just launched a missile). The AGM-12B had a 250 lb warhead, a range of 7 miles, and a weight of 571 pounds. The -12C carried a 1,000 lb warhead, had a 10-mile range, and weighed 1,785 pounds. Both models were built by the Martin Marietta Corp and the Maxson Electronic Corp.

However, the Bullpup was not to prove an effective weapon. It lacked the explosive strength to make it an effective weapon against such targets as bridges, the very type of objective that the missile had been designed to hit. Monograph 1 in the USAF south-east Asia Monograph Series, *The Tale of Two Bridges*, states: '. . .Captain Meyerholt was suprised to see no visible damage to the bridge as he guided his missile to a hit on the superstructure and pulled out to go around again. Like its precedessors, his missile had merely charred the heavy steel and concrete structure. When a second attack produced the same results, it became all too obvious that firing Bullpups at the Dragon (the Vietnamese name for the bridge at Thanh Hoa) was about as effective as shooting B-B pellets at a Sherman tank.'

ABOVE
Operating on the theory that you can never have too much firepower, the USAF tested gun pods on the inboard pylons of the Thud. This is a 20-mm cannon pod on an unidentified aircraft

LEFT
One of the early Thuds assigned to the 4th TFW, perhaps from the 335th TFS Detachment 1, has its ammunition loaded for publicity photographs

All the D models from the -5RE on, plus any earlier production aircraft that were later modified by the changes of TO D-687, were able to carry and launch two AGM-45A Shrike anti-radiation missiles on the outboard adapter developed for the Bullpup. So at least some of the effort in clearing the latter missile for Thud launches was not wasted. The AGM-45A was developed in 1961 for the specific purpose of tracking enemy radars. It had passive radar homing with a seeker head keyed to the threat frequency, a design feature which permitted little operational flexibility. It weighed 400 pounds, had a 19 to 25-mile range, travelled at Mach 2 and carried a fragmentation warhead detonated by a proximity fuse. Shrikes were built by Texas Instruments and the Univac division of Sperry.

The later Standard ARM (anti-radiation missile), the AGM-78B, entered service in 1968 with the F-105F Wild Weasels. It had a 15.5-mile range, hit Mach 2 peak speed and used broad-band passive radar homing. Additionally, the launch aircraft included a target identification and acquisition system built around an IBM 4-pounds digital computer. Standard ARM weighed 1,400 pounds and was built by General Dynamics and Maxson.

All of these weapons were launched through the AN/ASG-19 Thunderstick fire-control system, an integrated group of sub-systems – toss-bomb computer, attack and display unit and the R-14A radar – which calculated and directed the various modes of attack with the wide variety of available weapons.

Part of the developmental process which cleared specific missiles for launch was a determination of their trajectories after release and their stability along the initial part of the trajectory in close proximity to either the aircraft fuselage or wing. Computerized calculations of weapons' flight paths were the first step, using aerodynamic data from other missile and aircraft tests, but an unusual long-term armament test program was established by the USAF during 1968. More than 4,700 release trajectories of a variety of external stores – gun and rocket pods, bombs, missiles and fuel tanks – were simulated in wind-tunnel tests.

The key to the collection of that voluminous data – included many test points for an F-105D with external stores – was accurate simulation of the conditions of weapons release. Two kinds of tests were made. In one, miniature models of the stores were released from a model aircraft in an operating wind-tunnel and their separation and subsequent flight paths were photographed by high-speed cameras. Most of the tests, however, were carried out using a 'captive trajectory' system developed by ARO Inc., the operating contractor for AFSC's Arnold Engineering Development Center (AEDC), in Tullahoma, Tennessee.

This captive trajectory system was installed in the AEDC 4ft transonic wind tunnel. One part of the system was a quite conventional sting support for the model aircraft, holding the model on a cantilevered strut attached at the rear of the fuselage. The second part was a smaller, movable, strut which held the model store. It contained strain-guage instrumentation to measure the forces during separation. The store began the test at a position next to the aircraft which duplicated its actual position on the full-scale aircraft. Based on the forces recorded, a computer predicted a subsequent point on the trajectory and signalled the support system to move the model missile to that point. The forces were measured there and compared to the predicted value.

Disagreements between forces were resolved by movement of the store back along the trajectory until a point of agreement was found. The final trajectory was determined by these successive checks and showed clearly whether or not there would be interference when the store was released or ejected.

By the time this program was started by the Air Force, the F-105 had long been in combat, dropping the weapons and stores that had been cleared for use before then. AEDC tests on the stores of the F-105 included the determination of separation characteristics of the LAU-68A/A launcher for 2.75in unguided rockets, the SUU-45/A dispenser for bomblets, the CBU-34 dispenser for clustered fragmentation bombs, the A/B45Y-4 spray tank, and the AGM-12E Bullpup missile. As new weapons or stores were developed during the Vietnam war – such as the SUU-45/A dispenser pod – they were tried in miniature on the F-105 model in one of the AEDC tests, as well as on models of other aircraft in combat. The value of tests like those lay in the flight-test time they were able to save. Stores could be cleared on a preliminary basis for flight and release if the wind-tunnel tests showed safe separation. While the in-flight trajectory might differ somewhat from the wind-tunnel test flight path, the difference was generally minimal and the results were reliable.

For many years after World War II ended, bomb design lay stagnant in the United States. Little thought, if any, was given to the development of clean, stable shapes which would produce repeatable trajectories in flight, and reduce the dispersion pattern on impact. Even today, one glance at the ordnance load being carried by contemporary fighters should be a cause for considerable concern. The drag increment of externally hung weapons is formidable, and can substantially reduce the speed and range performance of an aircraft. Low-drag shapes had been studied and developed during the decade of the 1950s by both NACA and private industry, such as Douglas Aircraft Company, under contract to the military, but F-105s went into combat in Vietnam, a decade later, carrying bombs with less-than-minimum drag. One of these was the 750 lb M117 bomb. An issue of *Fighter Weapons Newsletter* (June 1964) describes the M117 and M118 bombs as a new series, with '...an external contour that is streamlined, resulting in low air resistance...' Maybe, but one combat report from 1966 stated that the F-105, armed with five Mk83 low-drag 1,000 lb bombs, burned several hundred pounds less fuel each hour than when the aircraft was loaded with a half-dozen 750 lb M117 bombs. Five bombs might normally be expected to produce less drag than six, depending on the way they were carried. However, the main factor in bombing is not drag, but weight of explosives on target, and five at 1,000 pounds is more than six at 750.

All of these weapons required a series of pylons, racks and adapters before they could be loaded aboard the fuselage and wing stations of the Thunderchief. Part of the design task for which Republic was responsible was the development of that ancillary equipment.

One of the 18th TFW Wild Weasels, an F-105F, equipped with ECM pods on outboard pylons and Standard ARMs on inboards, begins its take-off roll at Kadena

9
The Shapes of Thunder

Similar to every other military aircraft, the F-105 series was the subject of a number of modification programs. Perhaps the Thud had more than its share; there's never been a scorecard issued, and it would be most difficult to develop one. The F-105 modifications were, in main, intended to make it a first-line, combat-ready aircraft capable of performing its design or intended missions during its service with the USAF.

They began early, with the YF-105A, an aircraft which was to be only a geometric basis for what came afterwards. In airframe design changes, the A acquired a long nose, a higher tail, completely redesigned air intakes, a new powerplant and special fuselage shaping to smooth its fore-and-aft area distribution. Air refuelling capability was also added, as was a more sophisticated fire-control system.

The F-105B was modified by the incorporation of the AN/APN-105 Doppler radar all-weather navigation system. A new tactical thermo-nuclear weapon – designated TX-43 – had been developed at Los Alamos Scientific Laboratory and provisions to carry and release it had to be included in the B as a modification. A tow-target system was thrown in for good measure, making it possible for the F-105 to deploy a simple, delta-winged Dart target from an underwing pylon mount so that squadron pilots could practise air-to-air gunnery.

A powerplant change was made, replacing the J75-P-5 in the B-10 and B-15 production block aircraft with the J75-P-19, beginning with the B-20 production block and then converting the earlier models. New Goodyear brakes replaced an earlier type during B production and were also retrofitted on all aircraft. Then, towards the end of 1959, the Air Force asked for a group of changes, collectively to be done under Project Optimize. They

A few of the T-stick II aircraft were assigned to the Thud training wing at McConnell. Here's 61-0080 again, this time in the service with the 563rd TFS of the 23rd TFW

included modifications to the MA-8 fire-control system, the central air data computer, and the autopilot, to get them to do what they were supposed to have done. Project Optimize was planned as a four-month program, but it was drawn out and cost more money than was originally allocated.

The Thunderbird Thuds

One set of important, and very special modifications was made to nine F-105Bs. Ferried from the inventory at Seymour Johnson AFB, to Republic in October 1962, they were converted into mounts for the USAF's Thunderbird demonstration squadron. New flight controls were installed, a smoke system was added, the gun and its ammunition can were removed, some radio and electrical system changes were made and a baggage compartment was installed. On four of the aircraft a steel tail replaced the conventional structure; those four were to be available to fly the slot position, because of the

stresses imposed by the exhaust of the lead aircraft, and the solo position, because of the stresses of the 'knife-edge' maneuver.

Capt Jerry M. Shockley, who flew slot with the Thunderbirds, described the special F-105s in the *Fighter Weapons Newsletter* for June 1964. Wrote Shockley: 'Stability of the aircraft at high and low speeds is amazing; power response is great; flies good with stability augmentation in or out; and it's heavy. Low speed handling characteristics are very good (once you learn to use spoilers instead of rudder), and it's heavy.'

For the Thunderbirds' diamond formation, the average entry speed for looping manoeuvers was 450 KIAS (knots indicated air-speed); slowest over the top was 65, but was more normally 110 to 130 KIAS. Fastest solo speed was slightly above 600, depending on temperature, because the planes had to stay below Mach 1. Lowest of all air-speeds was experienced during the slow-speed Cuban Eight, where the indicators pegged at the minimum readable value of 40 KIAS over the top.

ABOVE
Thirty F-105Ds were modified to improve their bombing accuracy with a system designated Thunderstick II. The work was done at the factory, this is 61-0080, an F-105D-15RE, showing the enlarged dorsal spine that housed the new system

The last of the modified Bs was delivered to the Thunderbirds on 16 April 1964; within a month, however, all F-105s were grounded, following the break-up of one of the Thunderbird aircraft during a display at Hamilton AFB, California. The restriction was lifted in mid July, after inspection and fixes had been made, on all the B models and on some of the early Ds that had the same method of fuselage construction, to one key frame ahead of the wing.

The Thunderbirds kept the F-105s for only six displays. The model later equipped the 108th TFW of the New Jersey Air National Guard, a crack unit which kept the big Bs in service with a very high in-commission rate. Some were assigned to Nellis for instructor training, and those were later transferred to the single F-105 replacement pilot school, the 23rd TFW at McConnell AFB, Kansas, when Nellis began training instructor pilots for the General Dynamics F-111A.

The F-105D represented another major improvement, in terms of its installations. The thrust was increased by the installation of the -19W version of the big P&W J75 turbojet; it develops 2,000 pounds of additional thrust due to water injection head of the combustors. The conventional circular-display cockpit instruments of the B were replaced, in part, by an integrated instrument system featuring vertical tape read-outs. Because the D was heavier, than the B new wheels and brakes were needed and the main landing gear had to be strengthened. Fuselage and intake duct changes were made to handle the increased air-flow corresponding to the increased thrust.

Soon after all B and D models were grounded again in June 1962, the Air Force began Project Look Alike, whose goal was for as many as possible of the F-105s to be modified to a common configuration and for any necessary repairs to be carried out at the same time. The primary cause of the grounding were problems with the flight controls and chafing of fluid lines and wiring looms. Look Alike, like Optimize was planned on the assumption that it could be done quickly. In the event, it took two years and the costs rocketed.

Look Alike was completed in two phases, the first taking five months and involving the re-rigging of flight controls, the inspection of the chafed wires and lines and the completion of all modifications approved before the end of 1962. The second phase was the reworking or modifications of older F-105s to match the configuration of the 476th production article, the first F-105D-25RE. It was incidentally, a historical coincidence that the 'standardized' Republic Thunderbolt model of World War II was also a -25RE. Look Alike required approximately 5.4 million man-hours of direct labour, equivalent to 2,766 full-time specialists working for one year.

After the May 1964 grounding of all Thunderchiefs, caused by a series of accidents involving in-flight fires and explosions, all the D and F models were inspected carefully and released for flight, but the Air Force initiated a new series of modifications grouped in Safety Package I and Safety Package II. As a preparatory step to those programs, Republic sent teams of its own technicians to USAF bases, to train Air Force personnel in how to conduct proper, detailed and painstaking safety checks. These were primarily to detect leakage of fuel, oil and hydraulic fluids and were done during engine runs.

Packages I and II were composed of 21 separate modifications. Package I changed piping and tubing and reworked the fuel system to prevent the explosions and fires. Package II added engine ventilation scoops on the aft fuselage sides, to reduce the temperatures inside the shroud around the powerplant. The totals: 718 F-105s modified, at a labour cost of about 4,000 man-hours per aircraft. For statisticians, that's close to 2.9 million total man-hours, or 1,471 technicians working a standard 244-day year.

The F-105B Thunderbird team aircraft which crashed on 9 May 1964 broke up in the air during a high-speed pass and pull-up because a primary structural splice plate at the top centerline of the fuselage had failed due to

fatigue. The structure snapped, then the fuselage broke just forward of the leading edge of the wing. Project Backbone was the one which provided for the inspection of all F-105Bs and the replacement of the splice plate with one of a new design, less prone to fatigue failure.

Early combat experience in south-east Asia continued to emphasize the operational requirement for all-weather bombing and only the F-111 could meet the heartfelt need at the time. The inventory of those aircraft was so limited and their costs so high, that they were committed only on a small-force basis, and were never turned loose against targets in the North in quantity sufficient to prove their real worth or to make an impression on the North Vietnamese government. One feasible alternate seemed to be another Thud modification.

Thunderstick II for the Thud

The Air Force began the program in 1966, frustrated by the Thud's limited capabilities in battle once the sun had gone down, or the rains began. Thirty single-seat F-105Ds were selected to be modified with a much-improved attack system which would reduce the bombing CEP (Circular Error Probable) to meaningful numbers for bad-weather operations. The new bombing and navigation system was, quite naturally, named Thunderstick II, and was designed to give the F-105D a blind-bombing capability, as well as to improve its visual bombing from low altitudes.

BELOW
The T-stick II spine can be clearly seen from this angle. This is F-105D-20RE, 61-0110, of the 457th TFS at Carswell, taxiing after return from a practice bombing mission

Key sub-systems of the Thunderstick II system were:

ITT Avionics AN/ARN-92 Loran receiver, a digital unit to replace the Sperry AN/ARN-85 first specified and found wanting;
Autonetics R-14A radar, with its origainal vacuum tubes replaced by solid-state components;
Laboratory for Electronics AN/APN-131 Doppler radar;
Singer-General Precision inertial reference unit and gyro compass;
General Electric toss-bomb computer and AN/ASG-19 gunsight.

The Loran system was installed in saddleback fairing which extended from behind the cockpit of the F-105D to the vertical tail. It added 22 cubic feet of volume, made no significant change in the drag and improved the directional stability somewhat. The Loran antenna was molded into the canopy, just over the pilot's head.

Flight tests of the production system were begun at Eglin AFB during September 1969 and were completed on 7 November. The accuracy demanded in the contract was met, so the USAF was looking forward to a true round-the-clock attack capability featuring accurate blind conventional bombing.

The Thunderstick II system received only a limited evaluation under combat conditions in south-east Asia, wrote Gen William Momyer, but it required a high level of maintenance skills to keep the aicraft operational. Further, all the components of the system had to be working at peak performance to achieve the desired CEPs of less than 500 feet.

The Thunderstick II attack system showed promise for bombing rail yards and was used, according to Momyer, against the north-west railway line out of Hanoi for China. It was not used against the north-east line in time to escape the bombing halt which shut down all attacks north of the 20th parallel in 1968.

All 30 aircraft were finally completed by July 1971, five years after they were selected for the program. The reworked F-105Ds with their Thunderstick II/Loran systems never went to war in any quantity. One year after their completion, they were assigned, along with some other F-105 aircraft, to the 457th TFS of the reformed 301st TFW, an Air Force Reserve unit based at Carswell AFB, Texas. The 457th flew them until the end of 1982 and they are now in storage at MASDC.

Sharp-eyed spotters will have noticed that some of the otherwise standard F-105Ds have what appears to be a small saddleback fairing added to the top of the fuselage. This was the result of a hydraulic system modification, adding a back-up to the normal F-105 control systems which were in the belly. Relatively minor battle damage in the belly area often caused loss of control, followed almost immediately by loss of the aircraft.

The last 143 F-105D aircraft scheduled for production received the biggest modification of all: conversion to the two-place F-105F, the change which added a 31 inch fuselage extension for the second cockpit and a larger tailfin of greater height and increased chord. Some F

models were further modified to incorporate Wild Weasel equipment and they and others were still further modified into the F-105G Wild Weasel configuration.

A few F-105F aircraft were modified for all-weather, night, low-level radar bombing missions over North Vietnam and these extremely dangerous flights began on 26 April 1967. They were code-named Commando Nail and were part of the broad program of interdiction which carried various Commando codes. The pilots who flew the aircraft most frequently referred to themselves as 'Ryan's Raiders', after USAF General John D. Ryan, commander PACAF. These F-105Fs and improved radar-bombing systems, with the scope display expanded for clearer and sharper definition of the target. Further, weapons release was assigned to the back-seater, instead of being the pilot's function. The assumption was that the latter would be quite busy flying the aircraft. In 1968, Commando Nail F-105s were the primary all-weather and night fighter-bombers.

Another batch of only a few F-105Fs was modified by removing the rear seat and installing the powerful transmitters of the QRC-128 jammer. The equipment operated in the VHF range to blank out the voice link between ground controllers and MiG interceptors. These Thud modifications were code-named Combat Martin, and one of them is known to have been named, rather inelegantly, 'Fartin' Martin', by its pilot.

As a result of combat experience in south-east Asia, Republic and the Air Force made a number of changes and modifications in the standard D and F models. They included the installation of additional armour, passive and active fire-suppression systems and a passive explosion-suppression system for the fuel tanks, which were made self-sealing, and hardening the main fuel feed line. All the fuel cells were lined with new, orange-coloured polyurethane foam, a product developed by the Scott Paper Company and first used to protect drivers of racing cars at the Indianapolis Speedway. The foam was expected to reduce drastically the number of aircraft losses due to fire or explosion after fuel cells had been hit by incendiary ammunition.

Two relatively simple aerodynamic modifications were suggested as ways to add a significant amount of range performance. New wingtips, with increased area, were proposed; their additional area would reduce the wing's loading, and increase its aspect ratio. Both of those changes would improve the take-off, climb and cruise performance. The second suggestion was the addition of fore-and-aft strakes near the canopy, to keep the air-flow in that region smooth and further reduce the drag. Neither idea was followed through, although either – and especially the latter – would have been a quick and inexpensive field modification.

One of the most-requested modifications was the pilot recovery system (PRS). It came about because of the loss of control experienced after shrapnel from SAMs or AAA had knocked out the hydraulic system. Without its hydraulic pressure fixing the surface, the stabilator often slammed into a nose-high position, creating a sudden pitch-down force which pilots were powerless to counter.

TOP
A few F-105F models were modified by replacement of the rear seat with a QRC-128 jammer. It operated in the VHF range to jam the voice link between North Vietnamese ground controllers and their MiG-17 interceptor pilots. These were the Combat Martin Thuds, and shown here is 63-8291

ABOVE
The blade antenna of the Combat Martin jammer was installed on the dorsal spine must aft of the rear cockpit. Among F models known to have been so modified were 62-4432, 62-4444, 63-8291, and 63-8318

So they clamored for some emergency back-up system which would at least lock the stabilizer in an attitude to permit more-normal flight. Just another 5 or 10 minutes of flight time, they pleaded, would allow them to eject in a safe area.

Within six months, Republic engineers developed and delivered the first units of the PRS. As the pilots had suggested, it was a system which locked the stabilizer for normal flight. The pilot controlled the aircraft in pitch by varying the thrust and by symmetrical deflection of the trailing-edge flaps, which were electrically controlled. Lateral control came from differential deflection of the flaps and the use of the unboosted rudder.

In addition to these completed modification programs, there were a number of proposed schemes which never did get further than the paper stage. The following are some representative ones spanning a decade in the life of the F-105.

Strike-reconnaissance weapon system

In late September 1958, the Air Force defined a requirement for a tactical strike-reconnaissance weapon system designated SR-195. Republic's answer was AP 63-36, a growth version of the F-105D. It was to be built around advanced avionics, including an all-weather bombing system for all types of weapons. Its reconnaissance systems would be either electronic, via the installed avionics, or photographic, via a podded camera installation fitting in the bomb bay.

The company presented two versions, a normal and an economy model. The normal featured a new nose section to Station 300, with 32 inches added to the fuselage at that frame to provide space for a second cockpit. The wing-span was to be enlarged by 4ft by the addition of

new wing-tips. The canopy would be similar to that of the D with an extension to cover the second crewman. Advanced electronic equipment would be installed. The economy version was to be exactly the same, except that it was to retain the original wings, without the extensions.

Additionally, some design add-ons which had been considered for production aircraft were also proposed for the SR-195: boundary-layer control, saddle tanks, wrap-around tanks and a more powerful engine.

Installation of B-24 engine

Late in 1958, Pratt & Whitney proposed a new version of the J75, designated JT4B-24, with the same envelope dimensions and weight as the J75-P-19, but with greater thrust. Its 30,000 pound sea-level static rating was a major improvement over the 26,500 pounds of the -19W and promised positive performance increments in take-off, rate of climb, ceiling, acceleration and maximum speed.

With afterburner, the maximum speed was calculated to be Mach 2.29 at 36,000 feet and Mach 1.21 on the deck. The maximum sea-level rate of climb would have been 46,000 feet per minute, and the service ceiling would have increased to 48,000 feet. The clean airplane would have accelerated from Mach 0.8 to Mach 1.8 in 3 minutes, instead of the 4 that it took with the -19W engine. This B-24 engine was included in other proposals by Republic, but none of them went beyond paper studies.

British and French Thunderchiefs

In July 1960, Republic issued brochures for presentations of the F-105D to the French Armée de l'Air and the Royal Air Force of Great Britain. Both offers included on-site production, described the performance of the D from any of 425 standard NATO airfields and

Problems with the vulnerability of the dual hydraulic system, to enemy fire, led to a wartime modification that rerouted hydraulic lines through the small dorsal fairing on top of the fuselage

emphasized its ruggedness and its ability to carry 13,000 pounds of armament.

Costs, excluding the government-furnished aircraft equipment were between $1·3 and 1·4 million per unit.

The French proposal pointed out that a version of the J75 had been licensed for French production and was completely interchangeable with the J75-P-19W. The British were given the option of modifying the aircraft to take the Bristol Olympus B.01.22R, the engine developed for the ill-starred TSR-2 program. That power-plant gave 34,200 pounds of static thrust with afterburner and water injection and would have made a substantial improvement in the performance of the F-105D. Neither country accepted the proposal, however.

The Original F-105G

Before there was an F-105G Wild Weasel – in fact, before there was a firm contract for the F-105F – Republic engineers developed a new configuration with significant performance improvements and designated it F-105G. The proposal date was probably very early in 1962.

The reasons for the proposals were several. The USAF might decide against buying the F model, which didn't offer any substantial improvement over the D except for the two-man capability. Republic wanted to increase the service life of the F-105D, and to make it more reliable, more serviceable and more easily maintained: logistics support was a nightmare, because eight production blocks of D models had been built before that time.

The concept was to convert all of the 450 F-105D

End of the line for the Thud

aircraft in service, prior to the -31RE production block, consolidating eight different production models into one. It was a proposal comparable to that of Project Look Alike. The design would have featured the 31-inch fuselage stretch proposed for the F, installed a 220-gal fuel tank under the second cockpit, added saddle and area-rule bump tanks, installed the B-24 engine, strengthened the landing gear, increased the external fuel loading, made equipment changes for reliability and ease of maintenance and incorporated all the known fixes, retrofits, modifications and outstanding TCTOs (Time Compliance Technical Orders).

The cost of the conversion program was estimated at $321.3 million, or $714,00 per aircraft. Assuming Republic got a go-ahead from the Air Force in July 1962, the first aircraft could be accepted for conversion in January 1963 and delivered at the end of October. The program would have been completed by September 1965. However, the Air Force did buy the F model and the original G was never built.

Study for a speed record attempt

In February 1962, the Aeronautical Systems Division of AFSC asked Republic to see what possibilities the F-105D had of setting some new world speed records. An engineering and performance study showed that it could break several of the Class C-1, I records, particularly the 3km restricted altitude course record that had been set by a Navy F4H-1 Phantom II.

A production F-105D could almost do the job on a standard day at the 4,000 foot altitude of the course near Holloman AFB, New Mexico. A few simple

modifications would increase the speed to 976 mph and a little more thrust from the Pratt & Whitney engine would raise it to the magic 1,000mph mark. The simple modifications were to include removing the tailhook, sealing the aircraft, removing all protuberances, adding area-rule bumps ahead of the tail to decrease the drag and adding exit nozzle blisters similar to those of the Convair F-102 Delta Dagger, the so-called 'Marilyn Monroe mod', also for area-rule reasons. It was an interesting possibility, but for unrecorded reasons, the speed attempt was never made.

The F-105H Thunderchief

A few months later, Republic tried again to modify the Thunderchief, this time the F model. The new proposal, designated the F-105H, featured a new wing of 448 square feet in area, with folding wingtips. Its stabilator was increased in area to 133 square feet. The gun and ammunition were relocated in an inboard-pylon pod. The B-24 engine replaced the -19W, and additional fuel would have been housed in the bomb bay, under the second cockpit and in area-ruled tanks on wing pylons. A larger vertical tail, or a retractable ventral fin, or both, would have been designed. Weapons would be anything the D could carry, emphasizing the conventional types and the nuclear store would have been carried on a fuselage pylon. The landing gear was to be replaced by a tandem-wheel type; there would have been new trailing-edge and leading-edge flaps and actuating systems, a new aileron-spoiler system, new landing gear fairings and doors and new pylons.

This very extensive series of changes and additions was offered as a modification, but one engineer pointed out, in a contemporary memo, that it was really a new aircraft. The nose, center and rear fuselage sections would be new or extensively modified; the wing would be all new, as would the landing gear, the vertical fin and the stabilator.

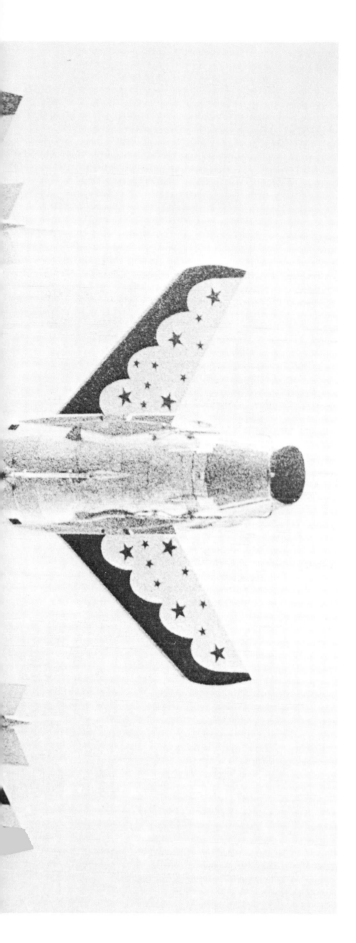

It's likely the Air Force saw the matter the same way and did not care to accept the proposal for the F-105H.

Advanced tactical avionics

In August 1964, Republic proposed installing advanced tactical avionics to modernize the entire F-105 fleet. The new systems, the five-volume company proposal stated, would extend Thunderchief missions, and improve its low-level penetration capability.

The major changes included an inertial measurement system, a dual-frequency, multi-mode radar, an automatic flight-control system, a digital central computer, a laser range-finder, a head-up display and a roller map in the aft cockpit of the F models. These installations would, it was believed, extend the inventory life through 1975.

The company proposed a three-phased program, with the first being a 15-month flight-test evaluation. Phase II would put a mixed D and F squadron, modified with production hardware, into an operational evaluation with PACAF, USAFE and CONUS units. The final phase was, of course, the modification of the fleet, with a completion date targeted in December 1968. The program would have no more than 100 F-105s in work at any time.

With a fleet of that size, and a war almost at hand, it would seem that the USAF decided against this program because it could not afford to take aircraft out of the inventory for anything but the most urgent reasons.

The F-105D-35RE

This effort was Republic's last valiant attempt to reopen the F-105 production line. In May 1968, the company presented its case for an advanced single-seat Thud based on the combat-proven D, adding the T-stick II bombing system and making a few other changes, including more fuel, and new pylons for weapons.

Only 344 F-105D aircraft remained at the beginning of May 1968, and they would all have been modified under the -35RE proposal. According to Republic's calculated performance and other data, the F-105D-35RE would have had a 20 percent payload improvement, a 27 percent range increase, a 73 percent decrease in vulnerable areas, more than 31 cubic feet of additional internal avionics volume, a 7g load factor with external stores and a superior tactical bombing system.

Fairchild Hiller, who had taken control of Republic, guaranteed 13-month deliveries at a unit cost of $1.8 million. It was a low-cost way of keeping a good aircraft in the inventory, but the USAF didn't see it that way. The F-105D-35RE became another in the long procession of paper planes which parade through the pages of aviation history.

Nine F-105B Thunderchiefs were modified to Thunderbird configuration, but an in-flight break-up grounded the type and the team. The Thunderbird Thuds were used in only six displays, and this outstanding marking scheme was short-lived

Citations

Medal of Honor recipients

The war in Vietnam produced 12 USAF recipients of the Medal of Honor, the highest military decoration awarded by the United States. Two were Thud pilots and both flew Wild Weasels.

Merlyn H. Dethlefsen

On 10 March, 1967, Major Dethlefsen (then Captain) was one of a flight of F-105 aircraft engaged in a fire suppression mission designed to destroy a key anti-aircraft defensive complex containing surface-to-air missiles (SAM), an exceptionally heavy concentration of anti-aircraft artillery, and other automatic weapons. The defensive network was situated to dominate the approach and provide protection to an important North Vietnam industrial center that was scheduled to be attacked by fighter-bombers immediately after the strike by Major Dethlefsen's flight. In the initial attack on the defensive complex the lead aircraft was crippled, and Major Dethlesen's aircraft was extensively damaged by the intense enemy fire. Realizing that the success of the impending fighter bomber attack on the center now depended on his ability to suppress effectively the defensive fire, Major Dethlefsen ignored the enemy's overwhelming firepower and the damage to his aircraft and pressed his attack. Despite a continuing hail of anti-aircraft fire, deadily surface-to-air missiles and counter-attacks by MiG interceptors, Major Dethlefsen flew repeated close range strikes to silence the enemy defensive positions with both bombs and cannon fire. His action in rendering ineffective the defensive SAM and anti-aircraft artillery sites enabled the ensuing fighter bombers to strike successfully the important industrial target without loss or damage to their aircraft, thereby appreciably reducing the enemy's ability to provide essential war material. Major Dethlefsen's conspicuous gallantry, consummate skill and selfless dedication to this significant mission were in keeping with the highest traditions of the United States Air Force and reflect great credit upon himself and the Armed Forces of his country.

Leo K. Thorsness

For conspicuous gallantry and intrepidity in action at the risk of his life and beyond the call of duty. On 19 April 1967, as pilot of an F-105 aircraft, Lieutenant-Colonel (then Major) Thorsness was on a surface-to-air missile suppression mission over North Vietnam. On that date, Lieutenant-Colonel Thorsness and his wingman attacked and silenced a surface-to-air missile site with air-to-ground missiles, and then destroyed a second surface-to-air missile site with bombs. In the attack on the second missile site, Lieutenant-Colonel Thorsness' wingman was shot down by intensive anti-aircraft fire, and the two crew members abandoned their aircraft. Lieutenant-Colonel Thorsness circled the descending parachutes to keep the crew members in sight and relay their position to the Search and Rescue Center. During this manoeuver, a MiG-17 was sighted in the area. Lieutenant-Colonel Thorsness immediately initiated an attack and destroyed the MiG. Because his aircraft was low on fuel, he was forced to depart the area in search of a tanker. Upon being advised that two helicopters were orbiting over the downed crew's position and that there were hostile MiGs in the area posing a serious threat to the helicopters, Lieutenant-Colonel Thorsness, despite his low fuel condition, decided to return alone through a hostile environment of surface-to-air missile and anti-aircraft defense to the downed crew's position. As he approached the area, he spotted four MiG-17 aircraft and immediately initiated an attack on the MiGs, damaging one and driving the others away from the rescue scene. When it became apparent than an aircraft in the area was critically low on fuel and the crew would have to abandon the aircraft unless they could reach a tanker, Lieutenant-Colonel Thorsness, although critically short of fuel himself, helped to avert further possible loss of life and a friendly aircraft by recovering at a forward operating base, thus allowing the aircraft in emergency fuel condition to refuel safely. Lieutenant-Colonel Thorsness' extraordinary heroism, self-sacrifice, and personal bravery involving conspicuous risk of life were in the high traditions of the military service and have reflected great credit upon himself and the United States Air Force.

Technical & Production Data

Production Data

Production F-105 aircraft carried three identifiers: RAC (Republic Aviation Corporation) number, Air Force serial number, and proudction block number. Additionally, successive numbers of aircraft were grouped under a common contract number, whether or not they were in the same production block.

Like everything else in the F-105 program, this numbering system took some time to settle down and straighten out.

The following statistics originated in Republic document 5-20.07 of 24 July 1963. Note that all serial numbers are inclusive.

Contract AF33(600)-22512, Project 57 (15 aircraft):

Block	YFA-1RE	AF 54-0098 & 54-0099
	B-1RE	54-0100 – 54-0103
	B-5RE	54-0104, 54-0106, 54-0107,
		54-0109, 54-0110
	B-6RE	54-0111
	JF-1RE	54-0105, 54-0108
	JF-2RE	54-0112

Contract AF33(600)-32216, Project 68 (65 aircraft):

Block	B-10RE	AF 57-5776 – 57-5784
	B-15RE	57-5785 – 57-5802
	B-20RE	57-5803 – 57-5840

Contract AF33(600)-34752, Project 79 (20 aircraft):

Block	D-1RE	AF 58-1146 – 58-1148
	D-5RE	58-1149 – 58-1165

Contract AF33(600)-34752, Project 80 (8 aircraft):

Block	D-5RE	AF 58-1166 – 58-1173

Contract AF33(600)-36687, Project 83 (68 aircraft):

Block	D-5RE	AF 59-1717 – 59-1757
	D-6RE	59-1758 – 59-1826

Contract AF33(600)-38927, Project 88 (139 aircraft):

Block	D-6RE	AF 60-409 – 60-426
	D-10RE	60-427 – 60-535
		60-5374 – 60-5385

Contract AF33(600)-40838, Project 90 (180 aircraft):

Block	D-15RE	AF 61-041 – 61-106
	D-20RE	61-107 – 61-161
	D-25RE	61-162 – 61-220

Contract AF33(600)-42709, Project 97 (195 aircraft):

Block	D-25RE	AF 62-4217 – 62-4237
	D-30RE	62-4238 – 62-4276
	D-31RE	62-4277 – 62-4411

Contract AF33(600)-42709, Project 31 (36 aircraft):

Block	1RE	AF 62-4412 – 62-4447

Contract AF33(600)-8154, Project 30 (107 aircraft):

No block given	AF 63-8260 – 63-8366

Production Units by Model and Block Number

Model	Block	Block quantity	Total
A	-1RE	2	2
B	-1RE	4	6
	-5RE	5	11
	-6RE	1	12
JF	-1RE	2	14
	-2RE	1	15
B	-10RE	9	24
	-15RE	18	42
	-20RE	38	80
D	-1RE	3	83
	-5RE	66	149
	-6RE	45	194
	-10RE	121	315
	-15RE	66	381
	-20RE	55	436
	-25RE	80	516
	-30RE	39	555
	-31RE	135	690
F	-1RE	36	726
	?	107	833

Total quantities produced of each model:

YF-105A	2
JF-105B	3
F-105B	75
F-105D	610
F-105F	143
Total	833

Performance

The simple question, 'How fast was the Thud?' loosens a flood of questions in response. 'Which model?' 'At what altitude?' 'On a cold or hot day?' 'Are you talking about a factory-fresh bird or a Thud after six months in Vietnam' 'What's it carrying and where?' By now the questioner has lost interest, which is why Republic and USAF publicists, who were asked the same questions, always said simply that the Thunderchief was a Mach 2 aircraft.

It was; the fact that it took four minutes of acceleration in full afterburner to reach that speed in level flight was never added, nor were any of the other qualifiers. Also, all of those factors questioned above cause changes in the performance, not only of the F-105, but of all aircraft.

In an effort to establish valid standards of performance for comparison, the USAF developed a series of Characteristics Summaries, a two-page tabulation of statistical and performance data for each of its aircraft in service. It is from these standard sets of data that the following performance figures are taken. They do not represent the best or worst performance, but they are real once-achievable performance figures, obtained during Category II flight tests. Also, a Category II test aircraft is different from one that has been soaking up moisture, sun and combat damage over a long period.

F-105B-20RE

Basis: Take-off weight (TOW), 46,998 lb; combat weight, 34,870 lb; fuel load, 2,510 gals, with 53.9 percent droppable and 0 percent protected; MK-28 in the bomb bay, 1,080 rounds of ammunition.
Combat radius: with 1,278 lb of fuel dropped prior to combat: 566 nautical miles at 508 knots average in 2.3 hours. If wing tanks were retained in combat, 646 nautical miles (nmi).
Ferry range: 1,935 nmi at 506 knots average in 3.81 hours, with 2,900 gals of fuel and at 46,979 lb (TOW).
Speed: Combat, 750 knots at zero ft, maximum; 1,195 knots at 36,089 ft altitude; basic, 750 knots at zero ft. All at maximum power.

Climb: 5,710 ft per minute (fpm) at sea level, TOW, military power; 33,800 fpm at sea level, combat weight, maximum power.
Ceiling: 32,750 ft, at 100 fpm rate of climb, TOW and military power; 48,100 ft, at 500 fpm rate of climb (R/c), combat weight, maximum power.
Take-off: 4,450 ft ground run; 6,220 ft to clear a 50 ft obstacle.
Stalling speed: 177 knots, power off, landing configuration, TOW.
Time to climb: 1.7 minutes, sea level to 35,000 ft, combat weight, maximum power.

F-105F

Basis: TOW, 52,077 lb; combat weight, 38,738 lb; fuel, 2,601 gals, 57.2 percent droppable, 0 percent protected; MK-28 in bomb bay, 1,000 rounds of ammunition.
Combat radius: 286 nmi at 518 knots average in 1.21 hours. If tanks retained, 459 nmi.
Ferry range: 1,300 nmi with 2,976 gals of fuel at 518 knots average in 2.52 hours at 52,095 lb TOW.
Speed: 681 knots at sea level; maximum, 773 knots at 36,000 ft basic, same as combat. All at maximum power.
Climb: 3,650 fpm at sea level, TOW and military power;

25,500 fpm at sea level, combat weight, maximum power.
Ceiling: 26,800 ft at 100 fpm R/c, TOW and military power; 45,100 ft at 500 fpm R/c, combat weight, maximum power.
Take-off: 5,490 ft ground run; 7,770 feet to clear a 50 ft obstacle.
Stalling speed: 185.8 knots, power off, landing configuration, TOW.
Time to climb: 15.9 minutes, sea level to 30,000 ft at combat weight, maximum power.

F-105G:

Basis: TOW, 54,580 lb; combat weight, 41,091 lb; fuel, 2,710 gals, with 57.2 percent droppable and 0 percent protected; 1 × AGM-78 and 2 × AGM-45A under wings, 581 rounds of ammunition.
Combat radius: 391 nmi at 514 knots average in 1.62 hours.
Ferry range: 1,623 nmi with 3,100 gals of fuel at 516 knots average in 3.15 hours at 51,139 TOW.
Speed: Combat, 681 knots at sea level; maximum, 723 knots at 36,000 ft altitude; basic, same as combat. All at maximum power.
Climb: 2,900 fpm at sea level, TOW, and military power; 23,000 fpm at sea level, combat weight, maximum power.

Ceiling: 24,600 ft at 100 fpm R/c, TOW, and military power, 43,900 ft at 500 fpm R/c, combat weight, maximum power.
Take-off: 5,800 ft ground run; 8,210 ft to clear a 50 ft obstacle.
Stalling speed: 187.6 knots, power off, landing configuration, TOW.
Time to climb: 28 minutes, sea level to 30,000 ft at combat weight, maximum power.

It's also important to note that the figures above are based on a standard day, when the sea-level temperature is 15°C (59°F). Hot days made things infinitely worse, as any pilot who flew out of Thailand can confirm.

F-105D-31RE:

Basis: TOW, 48,976 lb; combat weight, 35,637 lb; fuel load 2,710 gals, with 57.2 percent droppable and 0 percent protected; MK-28 in bomb bay, 1,000 rounds ammunition.
Combat radius: 543 nmi at 507 knots average in 2.23 hours. If tanks are retained, 676 nmi.
Ferry range: 1,917 nmi with 3,100 gals of fuel, at 507 knots average in 3.78 hours at 49,371 lb TOW.
Speed: Combat, 726 knots at zero ft; maximum, 1,192 knots at 36,089 ft, basic, same as combat. All at maximum power.

Climb: 4,650 fpm at sea-level, TOW, and military power; 34,000 fpm at sea-level, combat weight, maximum power.
Ceiling: 32,100 ft, at 100 fpm R/c TOW and military power; 48,500 ft at 500 fpm R/c, combat weight, maximum power.
Take-off: 4,270 ft ground run; 5,830 ft to clear a 50 ft obstacle.
Stalling speed: 180.6 knots, power off, landing configuration, TOW.
Time to climb: 1.75 minutes sea level to 35,000 ft, combat weight, maximum power.

Serial Numbers

Technical Order (TO) 1F-105-1133: *Modification and Redesignation of F-105F Aircraft to F-105G Configuration,* dated 23 February 1970, included the following information:

F-105F-1RE aircraft 62-4422 and 62-4434 are to be used for prototyping this TO. The 51 aircraft to be modified and redesignated are:

F-105F-1RE			
	62-4415	63-8284	63-8321
	62-4416	63-8285	63-8326
	62-4422	63-8292	63-8327
	62-4423	63-8296	63-8328
	62-4424	63-8300	63-8332
	62-4425	63-8301	63-8333
	62-4427	63-8302	63-8334
	62-4428	63-8303	63-8339
	62-4434	63-8304	63-8340
	62-4436	63-8305	63-8342
	62-4438	63-8306	63-8345
	62-4439	63-8307	63-8347

62-4442	63-8311	63-8350
62-4446	63-8313	63-8351
63-8265	63-8316	63-8355
63-8266	63-8319	63-8359
63-8281	63-8320	63-8360

TO 1F-105-1133C of May 1970 deleted two aircraft from the above list:

62-4415	and	63-8281

TO 1F-105-1133D of 01 July 1971 added these 12 aircraft to the F-105G program:

F-105F-1RE	62-4432	63-8276
	62-4440	63-8278
62-4443	63-8291	
	62-4444	63-8318
	63-8274	63-8336
63-8275	63-8363	

The final planned total of F-105G conversions was therefore 61 serially identified aircraft.

Tail Codes

The use of distinctive code letters or numerals on military aircraft, to distinguish a specific aircraft in a squadron, is as old as air combat itself. In World War I, fighters carried a numeral or letter, were frequently painted with distinctive colors and often bore additional, personal markings.

When the F-105 entered service, USAF aircraft were identified by the last five digits of the serial number. Thus, an early F-105B (serial number 54-0111) of the 4th TFW, a frequent subject of early publicity photos, carried a five-digit tail code of 40111. Additionally, the last three digits were repeated with a two-letter code, most commonly called a 'buzz number', emblazoned on both sides of the forward fuselage. F-105B 54-0111 also carried a buzz number of FH-111, FH being the identifier for the F-105 series. The Thud continued to carry that system of identification for several months after it entered combat late in 1964, but in about mid 1965, the buzz numbers were deleted, although the tail code number continued to be used.

After mid 1965, when the F-105s began to receive camouflage finish, the tail code numbers continued in use, but within PACAF sometime in 1967 or 1968, the numerical identifiers were dropped in favor of two letters, the first identifying the wing and the second the squadron. By mid 1968, TAC had adopted the system and USAFE followed in early 1970. Somewhere along the line, the tail code acquired a grander designation; it became, officially, the Distinctive Unit Identification (DUI).

In 1972, the USAF revised its maintenance procedures – another periodic exercise – to emphasize centralized work at the wing level, instead of at the squadron level. No longer were aircraft assigned by squadron. Consequently the DUI became wing identifiers, rather than wing plus squadron codes.

The war in south-east Asia presented a wealth of codes, some of which changed once or more during the years, and others which remained immutable then and until today. Some of the F-105 codes, collected by Frederick

W. Roos as part of *Research Project 7029* of the *American Aviation Historical Society,* included:

GA: 35 TFW, George AFB
GG: 35 TFS, 347 TFW, Yokota AB
GL: 36 TFS, 347 TFW
GR: 80 TFS, 347 TFW
HI: 466 TFS (AFRES), Hill AFB
JB: 17 WWS, 388 TFW, Korat RTAFB
JE: 44 TFS, 388 TFW
JJ: 34 TFS, 388 TFW
JV: 469 TFS, 388 TFW
MD: 561 TFS, 23 TFW, McConnell AFB

ME: 562 TFW, 23 TFW
MF: 563 TFS, 23 TFW
MG: 419 TFS, 23 TFW
RE: 44 TFS, 355 TFW, Takhli RTAFB
RK: 333 TFS, 355 TFW
RM: 354 TFS, 355 TFW
RU: 357 TFS, 355 TFW
TH: 457 TFS (AFRES), Carswell AFB
UC: 465 TFS (AFRES), Tinker AFB
WA: 57 FWW, Nellis AFB
WC: 66 FWS, 57 FWW, Nellis AFB
WW: 35 TFW, George AFB
ZA: 12 TFS, 18 TFW, Kadena AB

Surface Finishes

Until some time in 1962, production F-105s were delivered to the USAF with unfinished surfaces, other than for whatever treatment the aluminium and other materials had received during fabrication. Insignia and serials were applied in accordance with the standards of the day. An anti-glare panel in olive drab extended from the nose to the end of the canopy fairing.

Because of water damage to internal electronics and structure, 1962's Project Look Alike included a new surface finish which, it was hoped, would seal the seams and alleviate the damage. All F-105s modified under that program were finished with a heavily-pigmented aluminumized lacquer, which gave them a sleek, silvery-grey appearance.

After the first losses of F-105s to MiGs in combat during July, 1965, all were painted – as they became available for overhaul or major repair – with a standardized camouflage pattern in the now-familiar pale gray undersides and the tan-plus-two-tones-of-green upper surfaces. In the field, camouflage colors were hand-brushed or sprayed, and consequently, F-105s in service show considerable variation among individual aircraft at the same base. Some of the Thuds received a 'wrap-around' camouflage scheme, in which the upper-surface colors were extended around the fuselage and wings.

The standard insignia of the United States military aircraft was much too obvious to be continued in use after camouflage was applied. Other variations were tried, including a black star-and-bar not unlike the low-visibility dark gray insignia used on current USAF fighters. But that was not acceptable, then, and the USAF settled for a miniature of the standard insignia, with a 15 in diameter circle around the star.

Colored stripes had traditionally been used to identify separate squadrons within a wing and on the F-105 those colors were most commonly applied to the vertical tail. The USAFE Thuds used a triple diagonal stripe in the squadron colors and later the same geometry, but with the tricolor stripe, one band for each squadron color of red, blue, and yellow. Thuds went into combat wearing their squadron-color stripes, and even fancier ones, such as the broad starry blue tail topping of the 4th TFW, but in the war, those identifying stripes were painted over. Later, some squadrons painted the radar reflector on the nose landing gear with squadron colors, and that practice continued in peace-time.

The TAC insignia was applied to the vertical tail of all its aircraft beginning early in 1960. Squadron badges were sometimes used, such as the distinctive Indian head applied to the noses the F-105Bs of the 4th TFW.

During the war, individual aircrew applied names of artwork or both to their aircraft. The 355th TFW painted the names of its aircraft on the outer intake panel, generally on the left side only. The color field under the letters varied with the squadron: black for the 44th, red for the 333rd, blue for the 354th and yellow for the 357th. Artwork was generally applied to the sides of the fuselage, below the leading edge of the wing.

The 23rd TFW decorated all of its aircraft with a fierce shark-mouth that began just aft of the radome. Regulations, and good performance, require that radomes be kept in pristine condition. When aircraft from the 23rd were reassigned to the Georgia ANG, that outstanding organization kept the shark-mouth noses bright, wearing the distinctive marking as a reminder of the proud combat heritage of those Thuds.

In July 1970, officialdom took notice of the Thud artwork, and USAF ordered its removal. It took a while; unpopular directives can always be lost or misplaced. However, in November 1970 the word was sent out: General John D. Ryan, PACAF commander, was going to make his final inspection tour and the artwork had to come off now. It did.

After Gen Ryan left and when the Thuds returned to fighting north of the DMZ the artwork went back again. And it proved more durable than before, because units that received the aircraft after the end of the war kept the decorations throughout the life of the aircraft. Today, the long line of retired Thuds sitting in the desert sun at MASDC shows an occasional piece of artwork, surviving officialdom and generals (who probably wouldn't have objected anyway; their aircraft carried artwork in World War II).

AP Designations

First, the F-105 was *not* Republic AP 63-31. It was simply AP 63, maybe with a dash between the AP and the number, and maybe not. It depended on who was writing it. Further, the derivation of AP depends on who was remembering it. Most Republic people now call it Advanced Project. Older hands remember it as a holdover from the Seversky days, and the designation of Army Proposals.

During research for this book, the following AP 63 designations were discovered:

AP 63-10 Two-place, all-weather F-105
AP 63-19 Proposal for British, French and German co-production
AP 63-19E(?) Proposal to Canada for Strike Attack Interceptor Day Fighter Limited All-Weather F-105 with Orenda engine
AP 63-26 Proposal to Luftwaffe for F-105D version
AP 63-31 F-105D-31RE

AP 63-32 Proposal to Canada: F-105 with advanced Iroquois engine
AP 63-36 Proposal for SR-195 tactical strike – reconnaissance system

Additionally, these other AP designations were discovered:

AP 71 First RF-105 design proposal
AP 95 Air-to-surface ballistic missile
AP 96 Man-in-Space vehicle, proposed to USAF
AP 99 Strategic air-to-surface ballistic missile
AP 100 VTOL fighter-bomber
AP 106 Parametric study for VTOL aircraft

AP 95 was designed for operational use with the F-105, and was sized so that it could be carried internally in the bomb bay. It was Republic's first missile effort, made during 1957-58, and was formally proposed to the USAF on 17 April 1958. Republic quoted a cost of $74·5 million to design, develop, test and produce 200 units ($372,500 average unit cost).

Aerial Victories

During the war in Vietnam, F-105 aircrews shot down a total of 27½ MiG-17s, sharing one with the crew of an F-4D. The following listing is taken from *Aces & Aerial Victories,* published by the USAF Office of History in 1976.

Date	F-105 Aircrew	Parent Unit
1966		
29 Jun	Maj Fred L. Tracy	388 TFW
18 Aug	Maj Kenneth T. Blank	388 TFW, 34 TFS
21 Sep	1Lt Karl W. Richter	388 TFW, 421 TFS
21 Sep	1Lt Fred A. Wilson Jr	355 TFW, 333 TFS
04 Dec	Maj Roy S. Dickey	388 TFW, 469 TFS
1967		
10 Mar	Cpt Max C. Brestel*	355 TFW, 354 TFS
10 Mar	Capt Max C. Brestel*	355 TFW, 354 TFS
26 Mar	Col Robert R. Scott	355 TFW, 333 TFS
19 Apr	Maj Leo K. Thorsness, P†	355 TFW, 357 TFS
	Cpt Harold E. Johnson, EWO	355 TFW, 357 TFS
19 Apr	Maj Frederick G. Tolman	355 TFW, 354 TFS
19 Apr	Maj Jack W. Hunt	355 TFW, 354 TFS
19 Apr	Cpt William E. Eskew	355 TFW, 354 TFS
28 Apr	Maj Harry E. Higgins	355 TFW, 357 TFS
28 Apr	LtC Arthur F. Dennis	355 TFW, 357 TFS
30 Apr	Cpt Thomas C. Lesan	355 TFW, 333 TFS
12 May	Cpt Jacques A. Suzanne	355 TFW, 354 TFS
13 May	LtC Philip C. Gast	355 TFW, 354 TFS
13 May	Cpt Charles W. Couch	355 TFW, 354 TFS
13 May	Maj Robert G. Rilling	355 TFW, 333 TFS
13 May	Maj Carl D. Osborne	355 TFW, 333 TFS
13 May	Maj Maurice E. Seaver Jr	388 TFW, 44 TFS
03 Jun	Cpt Larry D. Wiggins	388 TFW, 469 TFS
03 Jun	Maj Ralph L. Kuster Jr	388 TFW, 13 TFS
23 Aug	1Lt David B. Waldrop, III	388 TFW, 34 TFS
18 Oct	Maj Donald M. Russell	355 TFW, 333 TFS
27 Oct	Cpt Gene I. Basel	355 TFW, 354 TFS
19 Dec	Maj William M. Dalton P**†	355 TFW, 333 TFS
	Maj James L Graham, EWO**†	355 TFW, 333 TFS
19 Dec	Cpt Philip M. Drew, P†	355 TFW, 357 TFS
	Maj William H. Wheeler, EWO	355 TFW, 357 TFS

† achieved in F-105F. All others in F-105D.
* Cpt Brestel downed two MiG-17s on the same flight.
**Crew shared the MiG-17, each man receiving credit for 0.5 MiG.

Index

Acknowledgements

A book is the product of many minds and hands. Research and writing of *F-105 Thunderchief* was simplified considerably by a large number of helpful friends, acquaintances, and (previously) complete strangers. They lent photographs, data, manuals, brochures, drawings, and – most importantly – their time. I'm most grateful to them all.

Former Republic employees: Paul S. Baker, Murray Berkow, Sidney P. Huey, George Hildebrand (since deceased), William J. O'Donnell, and Frank Strnad.

From Long Island's Cradle of Aviation Museum, a rough-cut gem now being assiduously polished by such dedicated folks as William K. Kaiser, Cdr, USN (Ret), the curator; Gary Hammond, the assistant curator; and Fred J. Freketic, Jr., photographer.

Former and current NACA/NASA specialists Lowell E. Hasel, H. Keith Henry, Laurence K. Loftin, Jr., Mark R. Nichols, M. Leroy Spearman, Phillip L. Stone, and Richard T. Whitcomb.

And these: Jack Broughton, Col, USAF (Ret), whose *Thud Ridge* is one of the literature's best war memoirs; Frank A. Carberry, photographer; Robert DeMaio, author of *A-10 Thunderbolt II;* Richard A. DeMeis, engineer and writer; Lou Drendel, of the indispensible . . . *in Action* series; Keith Ferris, the premier aviation artist; Jerry Geer, photographer; David A. Glow; MSgt B. D. Gordon, who convinced me that the 116th TFW was *really* Sierra Hotel; Randall D. Green; John F. Gulick, former director of communications for Fairchild Republic; George E. Haddaway, aviation advocate; Richard P. Hallion, reputable author and historian of the AF Flight Test Center; Fred Harl, photographer; Frank C. Hartman, photographer; and Paul Hoynacki, once an AF Captain flying Wild Weasel missions.

The list also includes: Bert Kinzey, of *Detail & Scale;* Thomas A. Koch, Major, USAF, of the Arnold Engineering Development Center; Raymond R. Leader, photographer; Don Logan, photographer; Mike Machat, brilliant young artist and illustrator; Jay Miller, of *Aerophile;* Dave Musikoff, who always finds something; Robert J. Pickett, trusting and generous photographer; Frederick W. Roos, researcher; Robb R. Satterfield, Maj, USAF (Ret), USAF an F-105 acceptance and flight test pilot; Jack T. Shea; Don Spering, of *Aircraft in Review*, air-to-air camera artist; James Perry Stevenson; John Weeks, the irascible resident 'Thud' expert at Fairchild Republic; and Fred Wolff, aviation illustrator.

Finally, one long-time friend and associate who always helps and who always requests anonymity.